Railways of Ayrshire

First ScotRail 380112 departs from Fairlie with the 07.15 Glasgow Central to Largs train (20 April 2012).

Railways of Ayrshire

GORDON THOMSON

THE CROWOOD PRESS

First published in 2016 by
The Crowood Press Ltd
Ramsbury, Marlborough
Wiltshire SN8 2HR

www.crowood.com

© Gordon Thomson 2016

All rights reserved. No part of this publication may be reproduced or transmitted in any form or by any means, electronic or mechanical, including photocopy, recording, or any information storage and retrieval system, without permission in writing from the publishers.

British Library Cataloguing-in-Publication Data
A catalogue record for this book is available from the British Library.

ISBN 978 1 78500 147 5

Acknowledgements
In putting this account of the history of the railways of Ayrshire together, I am grateful to many friends and acquaintances for supplying me with information, reminiscences and photographs of the county's railways. In no particular order, my thanks go to Jim Davidson, Andrew Arnot, Archie Thom, Arthur Wilson, Max Fowler, all members of the Ayrshire Railway Preservation Group, Terry Harrison and Stuart Rankin of the Glasgow and South-Western Railway Association. I have had fantastic support from my family, and especially from my wife Helen, in writing and preparing this book.

The contents of this book are intended to give a fairly detailed overview of the establishment, development and consolidation of the railways in Ayrshire, together with the current position and prospects for the future. This is based on personal observations and recording of the main-line railways as a resident in the county, and studying the plentiful literature previously written on railways in south-west Scotland, in particular, and Scotland in general. Also my involvement with the Ayrshire Railway Preservation Group for over thirty years has given me an insight into the industrial aspect of railway operation and the opportunity to play a very small part in its preservation.

Ayrshire's rich railway heritage has fascinated me for the three decades and more that I have lived here, and through the pages of this book I hope to inspire a similar fascination.

Finally, my thanks to The Crowood Press for giving me the opportunity to put my thoughts into print.

Except where otherwise stated, photographs are from the author's collection

Typeset by Jean Cussons Typesetting, Diss, Norfolk
Printed and bound in Malaysia by Times Offset (M) Sdn Bhd

Contents

Introduction		7
Chapter 1	Early Beginnings: to 1850	9
Chapter 2	Glasgow and South-Western – the Network Evolves: 1850–80	23
Chapter 3	Later Additions: 1880–1923	51
Chapter 4	The London, Midland and Scottish Railway (LMS) Era: 1923–48	65
Chapter 5	Nationalization and British Railways: 1948–98	72
Chapter 6	Privatization	106
Chapter 7	Present Day	119
Chapter 8	Industrial Railways and Preservation	129
Appendix I: Ayrshire's Railway Stations: Opening and Closure Dates		151
Appendix II: Railway Abbreviations		155
Bibliography		156
Index		157

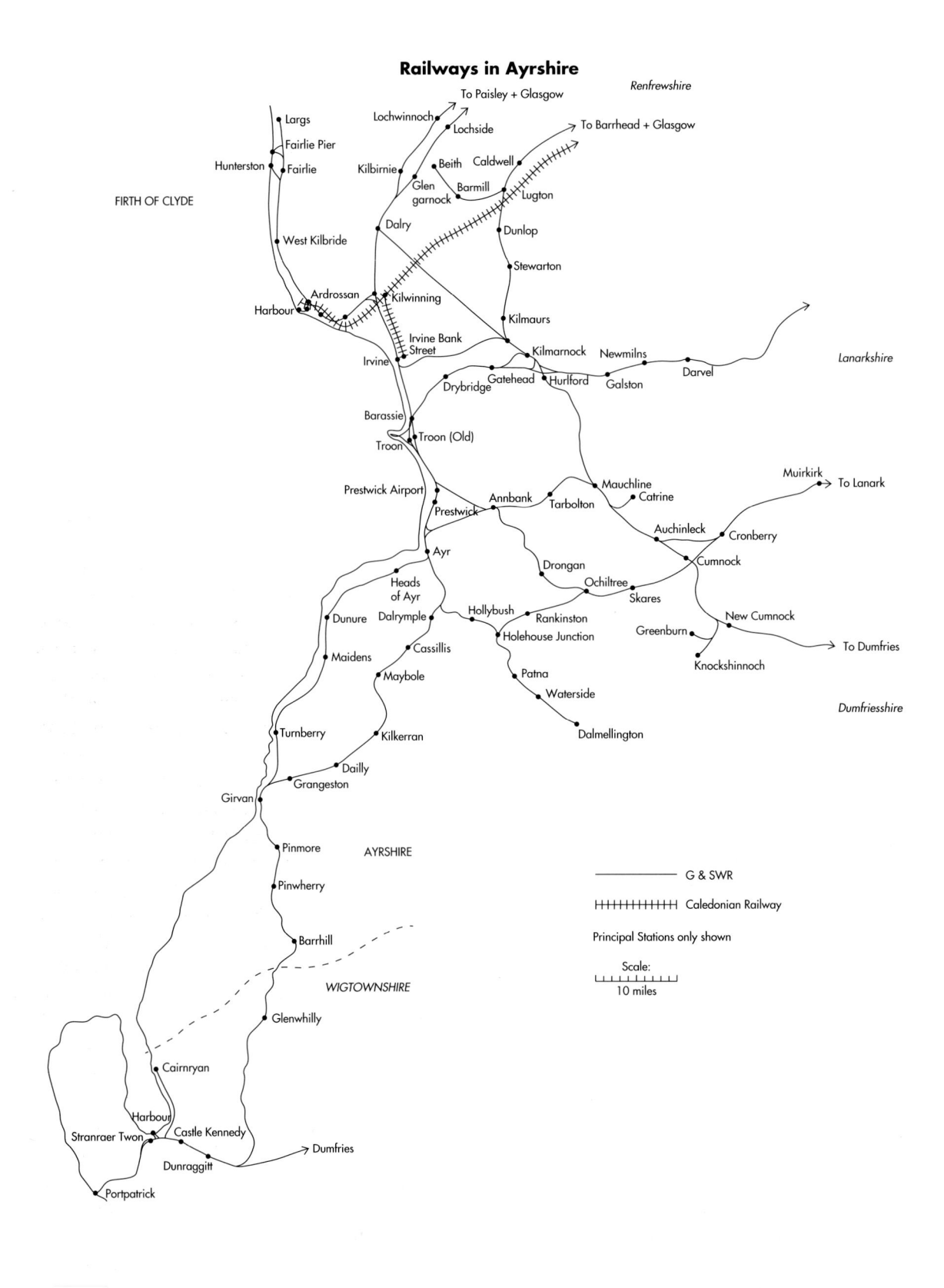

Railways in Ayrshire

Introduction

Ayrshire – the name suggests a county in the lowlands of Scotland, and will not mean much to the average British railway enthusiast. So exactly where is it and what attraction does it hold for the visitor, and in particular the railway enthusiast?

Ayrshire is located immediately to the south-west of Scotland's largest city, Glasgow, on the shores of the Firth of Clyde, the shoreline extending 84 miles from Skelmorlie in the north to just north of Cairnryan, 6 miles from Stranraer. The county covers approximately 1,140 square miles (2953km^2). Its population totals 366,800, a little more than the populations of Coventry, Cardiff or Bradford. The traditional county town is Ayr (population 46,900), with other principal towns Kilmarnock (population 46,200) and Irvine (population 39,500), which are the administrative centres for the local authority areas of South Ayrshire, East Ayrshire and North Ayrshire, respectively. The county encompasses the Isles of Arran, Great Cumbrae and Little Cumbrae, as well as the uninhabited island of Ailsa Craig. Anywhere on the coastline offers superb views over the Firth of Clyde towards Arran and beyond.

Inland, Ayrshire has borders with the old counties of Renfrewshire, Lanarkshire, Dumfriesshire and Wigtownshire. The countryside in those areas is very unspoilt, consisting of gentle hills and upland moorland, rising in the south-east to the scenic Galloway hills. It is in these hills that we reach the highest point in Ayrshire.

The economics of Ayrshire are (or were) a curious mix – steelmaking, coal-mining and large-scale manufacturing, going hand in hand with agriculture. There were, and still are, rich coal deposits, leading to large-scale coal-mining for the past 200 years. There was steelmaking in the north of the county, at Glengarnock, into the 1980s. Coal-mining, traditionally deep mines but now opencast, continues. There was much 'production line' manufacturing also, particularly in Kilmarnock, such as Glenfield & Kennedy (valves, pipes and equipment for the water industry), Massey Ferguson (tractors), Blackwood Morton Carpets (more commonly known as BMK – Blackwood Morton, Kilmarnock), Andrew Barclay, Sons & Co. (locomotive manufacturers) and the world-famous Johnnie Walker whisky, which originated in the town. Just about all of these industries have gone. Agriculture contributes immensely to Ayrshire's economy; it is one of the most fertile areas of Scotland. The famous 'Ayrshire tatties' are grown near the coast, and other root vegetables, together with strawberries and raspberries, are extensively cultivated. Cattle farming is also a large element, producing both beef and milk, with sheep farming on the higher ground.

INTRODUCTION

The important international airport at Prestwick remains in operation, a significant link for both passenger and freight traffic. There was also aircraft manufacturing at Prestwick, which ceased in 1998; but components and other elements continue to be produced there.

Having such a long coastline, there are many harbours both large and small. From the north, there are harbours at Largs, Fairlie, Ardrossan, Irvine, Troon, Ayr, Dunure, Girvan and Ballantrae – all still function: Largs (for Cumbrae), Ardrossan (for the Isle of Arran), and Troon (for Belfast – summer only) are ferry ports; commercial traffic still uses Troon and particularly Ayr, and all handle sea fishing.

Several world-famous people have their origins in Ayrshire. The best known is Scotland's most famous poet, Robert Burns (1759–96), who was born and brought up in Alloway, a couple of miles south of Ayr, and spent most of his life in the county. John Dunlop (1840–1921), who invented the pneumatic tyre, came from Dreghorn, near Irvine. Scottish legend Robert the Bruce (1274–1329) was reputed to have been born at Turnberry Castle, near Girvan. Bill Shankley (1913–81), distinguished and highly successful Liverpool FC manager in the 1960s and 1970s, came from the mining community of Glenbuck, near Muirkirk.

Sir Tom Hunter, wealthy entrepreneur and philanthropist, is based in Ayrshire, and Scotland's current (2015) First Minister, Nicola Sturgeon, is from Dreghorn near Irvine. Sam Torrance, a successful professional golfer, and ex-Ryder Cup captain, hails from Largs. Numerous Scottish football players from Ayrshire have worn the colours of their clubs and country with distinction.

Ayrshire must have the highest density of golf courses per square mile in the United Kingdom – the game is played extensively. The world-class links courses at Turnberry (established by the railway with its famous hotel) and at Royal Troon regularly host the biggest and most prestigious tournament in the world: the Open Golf Championship.

In the early 1800s, Ayrshire was already established as a prosperous, mainly rural agricultural county. The realization that there was abundant coal and, to a lesser extent, iron-ore deposits to be exploited, together with the coming of the industrial revolution generally throughout the United Kingdom, rendered the area wide open to the 'railway mania' that swept Britain in the mid- to late 1800s. The proximity of the county north to Glasgow and south to Carlisle (and thence south) made Ayrshire an attractive proposition for early railway developers.

So that's a brief overview of the county of Ayrshire – what of its railways? That is the purpose of this book, so let's get started.

Note: in 1965 'British Railways' was rebranded as 'British Rail'. At the same time, a move was made from the 12-hour clock to the 24-hour clock for the expression of train times; this convention has been followed here.

CHAPTER 1

Early Beginnings: to 1850

Early Wagon-Ways

The first railways, not in the sense we know nowadays but more accurately described as 'wagon-ways', appeared in the district round the county town of Ayr, to link the primitive early coal-mines in the districts of Auchincruive and Annbank with the town and harbour. There is little or no written record of these early wagon-ways, only a study of old maps prove their existence, plus some remains of structures such as bridges and embankments, now long reclaimed by nature. There is certainly no photographic record. There appear to have been several in existence – mostly short in length and in the time they were in use. The biggest and longest appeared to be one that eventually stretched from Ayr Harbour all the way to Annbank, some 5 miles, with various spurs and short branches to various small coal-mines. All were powered by horse and would have had cast-iron rails of undefined gauges. The technology of rail transport had thus been proved, and these early wagon-ways were shortly to be superseded by the real thing.

Kilmarnock and Troon

A little further north from Ayr, the Kilmarnock and Troon Railway is generally regarded as one of the

Kilmarnock; BR Standard 5MT 4-6-0 73102 with a train for Glasgow St Enoch. ARTHUR WILSON

Gatehead; 09.10 Ayr–Carlisle (19 May 1979).
MATT MILLER

first railways to be built in Scotland, if not the United Kingdom; certainly the first in Scotland to be built under an Act of Parliament.

In the early 1800s, the fourth Duke of Portland operated a number of coal-mines around Kilmarnock. Much of the output was exported by sea from the nearby harbour at Troon. An easy and efficient way of transporting coal to Troon was required, so, in 1807, the Duke of Portland appointed William Jessop to survey a route for a plateway or railway. An Act of Parliament was obtained the following year. Work was duly started to build the line over the undemanding terrain between the two towns, and the new line was completed and ready for use in 1812. The rails were cast-iron angles taking wagons with flangeless wheels that were drawn by horses. The rails were laid on stone blocks with a gauge of 4ft (1.2m), there being no standard gauge at that time. The new railway cost £40,000 to build and was 9½ miles (15km) long.

In 1813, a horse-drawn passenger coach was built and carried the name 'Caledonian'; this almost certainly was the start of rail-passenger services in Scotland. This commenced carrying passengers

Gatehead; former station and signal box (7 July 1987).

between the two towns on 1 May 1813 and was run by William Wright of Kilmarnock. The coach ran only in the summer months on Tuesdays, Thursdays and Saturdays, with the return fare being two shillings and sixpence (12.5p nowadays), although a reduced fare of one shilling and sixpence was charged if you travelled on the roof of the coach.

Propulsion by steam was being developed by George Stevenston in the north-east of England, and in 1817 the railway ordered a locomotive, at a cost of £750, to try out on the railway. The new locomotive duly arrived and was named 'The Duke'. It was put to work and caused quite a stir in the area, a sight the likes of which had never been seen before. It was the first steam locomotive to work in Scotland. It was able to haul loads of up to 30 tons (30,480kg) of coal at 5mph (8km/h). The one drawback was that the cast-iron rails frequently broke under the weight of the locomotive, adding considerably to the maintenance of the railway. The Duke was withdrawn from service in the 1830s and was scrapped for the sum of £13.

Two of the bridges on the route are of interest. The first was at the village of Drybridge. The tiny village took its name after the railway was built, as at the time it was unprecedented for a bridge to span anything other than water – hence it was a 'dry bridge'. The other is found near the village of Gatehead, at the Laigh Milton Mill. It is a four-arch-span viaduct over the River Irvine, probably the first

Drybridge; BR class 56 passes the station site with a coal train (c. 1992). ARCHIE THOM

Drybridge; BR 47488 passes the former station with the 11.00 Stranraer–London Euston (24 June 1987).

Laigh Milton Viaduct, Gatehead (12 September 2014).

EARLY BEGINNINGS: TO 1850

LEFT: *Barassie; Kilmarnock line platforms, class 107 DMU on the 09.10 Ayr–Carlisle (10 April 1976).* JIM DAVIDSON

BELOW: *Barassie; EWSR 66003 comes off the Kilmarnock line with cargo-wagons from the Caledonian Paper Mill (3 May 2002).*

EARLY BEGINNINGS: TO 1850

Old wagon-way rails, Laigh Milton Viaduct, Gatehead (12 September 2014).

The Kilmarnock and Troon Railway (K&TR) continued in use in its original form until 1846 when the railway revolution caught up with it. New lines were being built all over the UK and in that year the Kilmarnock and Troon Railway Act was passed, which enabled the Glasgow, Paisley, Kilmarnock and Ayr Railway Company to integrate the line with the railways that were being developed to those towns. The K&TR was rebuilt to standard gauge, double-track and re-aligned in places. By 1850 the railway had become part of the newly formed Glasgow and South-Western Railway (G&SWR), and had a local passenger service between Kilmarnock and Ayr, with passenger stations at Gatehead (3 miles from Kilmarnock) and Drybridge (5 miles). It joined the Glasgow to Ayr line at Barassie, and continued on its own way from there to its terminus at Troon Harbour. In 1846, the Kilmarnock and Troon Railway was leased (for 999 years) to the Glasgow and South-Western Railway, but finally, in 1899, the G&SWR purchased the line outright.

railway viaduct in the world. It was superseded by a new alignment of the railway in 1846 and became derelict. After 150 years of neglect, and almost on the point of collapse, it was refurbished as a visitor attraction in 1996.

BR class 101 and class 126 DMUs meet at Barassie (19 May 1979). MATT MILLER

The Links to Glasgow

In the early 1800s, just before the coming of the railways, canals were the favoured method of transport. A canal was built from Glasgow to Paisley and on to Johnstone in Renfrewshire, with the ultimate goal of Ardrossan Harbour, in Ayrshire. At this point 'railway mania' took over, and the plan was revised to include building a railway from the canal basin in Johnstone to Ardrossan. However, this line was opened in 1831, but was only built from Ardrossan to Kilwinning, at 4ft 6in gauge. It used horse haulage, in common with the Kilmarnock and Troon Railway. It was at this time that the development of the railways in south-west Scotland began to take off, with the formation in 1837 of the Glasgow, Paisley, Kilmarnock and Ayr Railway, which aptly described its ambitions. The proposed line struck westwards from Glasgow to Paisley, then swung south-west towards Ayrshire, entering the county at Beith. The line was opened in stages:

- Ayr to Irvine opened 5 August 1839.
- Irvine to Kilwinning, 23 March 1840.
- Glasgow to Paisley (joint line with the Caledonian Railway), 14 July 1840.
- Kilwinning to Beith, 21 July 1840.
- Beith to Paisley, 12 August 1840 – line complete.

Dalry; LMS Hughes 'Mogul' calls with a Glasgow St Enoch to Ayr train (late 1950s). BILL HAMILTON

The line passed through several villages and towns on its way from Paisley to Ayr, and by 1923 there were stations at (miles from Glasgow St Enoch) Johnstone (11), Cochrane Mill (later Milliken Park) (12¼), Howwood (13¾), Lochside (16½), Beith North (18½), Glengarnock (20½), Dalry (23¼), Kilwinning (26¾), Bogside (29), Irvine (30¼), Gailes (32), Barassie (33¾), Troon (35), Monkton (37¼), Prestwick (38¼), terminating at the orginal passenger terminus on the north side of the River Ayr at 40¾ miles from Glasgow (St Enoch). Most of these stations are still open to passenger traffic.

Glengarnock; First ScotRail 156477 passes with a Stranraer to Glasgow Central train (4 October 2012).

Kilwinning; class 107 DMU taking the Largs line (August 1978). MATT MILLER

CENTRE LEFT: *Kilwinning; EWSR 60500 with the Prestwick Airport to Grangemouth empty aviation fuel tankers (13 November 2007).*

CENTRE RIGHT: *Bogside; Network Rail HST 'New Measurement Train' passing the site of the old station (23 September 2014).*

RIGHT: *Irvine; class 101 DMU on an Ayr to Glasgow train during station refurbishment, just prior to electrification (8 August 1986).*

Gailes; 60021 with the Prestwick Airport to Grangemouth empty aviation fuel tankers (5 July 2002).
MAX FOWLER

ABOVE: *Barassie; 26036 passes with an engineers' train (12 July 1990).*

LEFT: *Troon (old): class 126 'Swindon' DMU 126413 heads down the Troon avoiding line past the site of the original Troon station with the Glasgow Central to Stranraer train (20 November 1982).*
ARTHUR WILSON

EARLY BEGINNINGS: TO 1850

Troon; BR 'Clan' 72005 passes Troon's original station with a Glasgow–Carlisle parcels train (late 1950s). BILL HAMILTON

LMS 'Jubilee' class 45673 passes the site of Monkton Station with an Ayr–Glasgow St Enoch train (late 1950s).
BILL HAMILTON

Ayr Goods Station, on North Harbour Street, formerly the North Side passenger station, closed in 1973 (May 1972).
ARTHUR WILSON

Prestwick; 156447 calls at Prestwick with a Girvan–Kilmarnock train (10 August 2012).

Ayr; LMS 'Black 5' 44871 with the 'Great Britain VI', arrived from Stranraer (30 April 2014).

RIGHT: Ayr Goods Station and bridge over the river Ayr (November 1974). ANDREW ARNOT

Newton-on-Ayr; 37xxx heads up the Annbank line with tankers (April 1974). ARTHUR WILSON

Stevenston, looking east, in its modernized, post-electrification form (1 December 2008).

Kilwinning to Ardrossan

The short railway from Ardrossan to Byres on the outskirts of Kilwinning did not long remain a small, isolated stretch of railway. By 1840, the line had been rebuilt to standard gauge, double-track, and extended into the town of Kilwinning, making a junction with the newly constructed Ayr to Paisley railway. Stations were provided at Stevenston, Saltcoats and Ardrossan, the line terminating at Ardrossan Harbour (subsequently named Winton Pier). This railway opened at the same time as the main line, on 12 August 1840. At Kilwinning, a short chord (a length of railway to connect two other

26043 entering Barassie Yard with an engineer's train. The Troon loop line (the main Glasgow to Ayr railway) curves off to the right, with the line from Kilmarnock. The original main line continues straight ahead, now cut back and known as Barassie Yard (26 June 1987).

Ardrossan South Beach, post-electrification form; 380111 calls with a Largs–Glasgow Central train (14 August 2012).

longer, separate railways) was built to enable trains from the Ayr direction to run directly to Ardrossan, from Byrehill Junction to Dubbs Junction. Along this short length of railway, at Blacklands Junction, an industrial railway branched off to the Eglinton Ironworks and beyond. This was known as the Doura branch. This branch ultimately extended to Perceton, east of Irvine, serving the Eglinton Ironworks and several coal-mines along its way. It was purely a mineral railway, and never carried passengers.

To Kilmarnock

The 'branch' from Dalry to Kilmarnock, a distance of 11 miles, was opened on 4 April 1843; in truth this line was in all respects a main line. Stations were provided at Montgreenan and Cunninghamhead (initially named Stewarton). The line was relatively easy to build, being through undulating countryside with no special engineering required, apart from a few viaducts over rivers.

The station building at Montgreenan (Dalry to Kilmarnock line), closed in 1956, now a private residence.
STUART RANKIN

Was there ever a railway station here? Cunninghamhead (Dalry to Kilmarnock line) (6 May 2008).

Crosshouse Station site, left hand to Irvine, right hand to Dalry; overbridge from the east (12 May 2007).

Cross-County

A new railway, 5¼ miles long, from Crosshouse (1¾ miles north of Kilmarnock on the Dalry line), to Irvine was opened on 24 May 1847. The line was double-track and eventually had several mineral branches to various collieries, with passenger stations at (miles from Kilmarnock) Springside (4 – opened much later on 1 June 1890) and Dreghorn (5¼). This was an especially useful, short, cross-country railway, enabling trains from the port of Ardrossan to get to Kilmarnock easily and quickly

Auchinleck; 20020 passes with a goods train (6 August 1978). MATT MILLER

BR 'Clan' 72005 'Clan MacGregor' passes Auchinleck with a goods train (late 1950s).
BILL HAMILTON

via the Dubbs Junction–Byrehill Junction curve and Irvine. Off this line were several small coal-mines, which added to the traffic that used the line, although most had gone by the early 1920s. Again, there were no major engineering structures required, and the railway was completed relatively quickly.

Eastwards from Kilmarnock lay the valley of the River Irvine, in which lay the towns of Galston, Newmilns and Darvel. They were not to be left out, and a railway was built from the main line to the south at Hurlford (1¾ miles south of Kilmarnock), initially as far as Galston (5½) on 9 August 1848, eventually extended to Newmilns (7¼ miles) on 20 May 1850 and Darvel (9¼ miles) – much later on 1 June 1896.

Also, on 9 August 1848, a 10-mile long railway was opened from Auchinleck on the main line south, to the moorland town of Muirkirk, where coal-mining and iron-founding were being established. Again the line was laid double-track in anticipation of the traffic expected. Stations were provided at the communities of Commondyke (2¾ miles from Auchinleck), Lugar (3¾) and Cronberry (4½), with the terminus at Muirkirk (10¼). There were short branch lines provided to Lugar Ironworks and Gasswater Coal-Mine.

Highland Railway 'Jones Goods' no.103 at Cronberry with a railtour (April 1962). BILL HAMILTON

CHAPTER 2

Glasgow and South-Western – the Network Evolves: 1850–80

The Main Lines to Ayr and Kilmarnock and Beyond

Until 1840, the railways in south-west Scotland, and in Ayrshire in particular, were essentially local affairs. The various promoters saw the 'bigger picture' beyond linking the various towns in Ayrshire to Glasgow (and vice versa), to expanding south to the important town of Dumfries and linking into the English network at Carlisle. Rival companies were planning a similar line from Glasgow, southwards via Clydesdale, Beattock and Liddlesdale to Carlisle. This was a more direct route south, but after leaving the Lanarkshire town of Motherwell, there were no major centres of population until Carlisle was reached.

LMS 'Princess' class 46201 'Princess Elizabeth' leaves Kilmarnock on the Dalry line with a parcels train for Glasgow (late 1950s).
BILL HAMILTON

BR class 45 no.22 arrives at Kilmarnock with an express for London St Pancras (21 September 1973). JIM DAVIDSON

The railway from Glasgow had already reached the major towns of Kilmarnock and Ayr by 1843, via Paisley. This, the Glasgow, Paisley, Ayr and Kilmarnock Railway, split at Dalry, one line continuing inland to Kilmarnock, the other heading for the Clyde coast and finishing in Ayr. The promoters of the new line, the Glasgow, Dumfries and Carlisle Railway Company, saw Carlisle and the Anglo-Scottish traffic as its goal southwards, and upon authorization in July 1846, wasted no time in getting the new line built. Construction started at both ends; the various sections were completed as follows:

- Kilmarnock to Auchinleck opened 9 August 1848.
- Dumfries to Gretna Junction (9 miles north of Carlisle) opened 23 August 1848.
- Closeburn to Dumfries opened 15 October 1849.
- Auchinleck to New Cumnock opened 20 May 1850.
- New Cumnock to Closeburn opened 8 October 1850: line complete.

Bowhouse; Virgin class 57 with the diverted 11.25 Glasgow Central–London Euston (March 2004).
MAX FOWLER

BR class 47 approaching Mossgiel tunnel with a Glasgow to Nottingham train (May 1980). MATT MILLER

LMS class 5MT 'Black 5' 037.5M approaching Mauchline from Ayr with a goods train (early 1960s). BILL HAMILTON

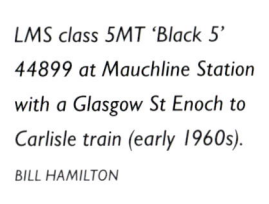

LMS class 5MT 'Black 5' 44899 at Mauchline Station with a Glasgow St Enoch to Carlisle train (early 1960s).
BILL HAMILTON

GLASGOW AND SOUTH-WESTERN – THE NETWORK EVOLVES: 1850–80

Mauchline Station; island platform building from the north (September 1971).
STUART RANKIN

BELOW: *BR class 45 crossing Ballochmyle Viaduct with a train for Carlisle and beyond (28 May 1975).* JIM DAVIDSON

Mauchline Station from the south (September 1971).
STUART RANKIN

Auchinleck; 156433 calls with the 1307 Glasgow Central–Carlisle train, not long before the station building and signal box were demolished (22 June 1990).

From Kilmarnock to Gretna Junction (7½ miles north of Carlisle, just over the Border) was 84 miles. Intermediate stations were provided at (south from Kilmarnock) Hurlford, Mauchline, Auchinleck, Old Cumnock, New Cumnock, and (in Dumfriesshire) Kirkconnel, Sanquhar, Carronbridge, Thornhill, Closeburn, Auldgirth, Holywood, Dumfries, Racks, Ruthwell, Cummertrees, Annan, Dornock, Rigg, and Gretna Green.

RIGHT: Freightliner 66551 passes the site of Brackenhill Junction with a southbound coal train (1 April 2014).

New Cumnock: 20119 and 20122 over Polquhap summit with a coal train from Knockshinnoch to Ayr Harbour (17 August 1990).

Virgin trains class 57 and class 390 'Pendolino' approach Polquhap summit with a diverted Glasgow Central to London Euston train (14 April 2006). MAX FOWLER

47536 heads the diverted 14.10 Glasgow Central to London Euston train past the site of New Cumnock station (16 April 1989). ARTHUR WILSON

The date of 8 October 1850 not only marked the completion of the new Anglo-Scottish main line, but also the amalgamation of the Glasgow, Paisley, Ayr and Kilmarnock Railway and the Glasgow, Dumfries and Carlisle Railway to form the Glasgow and South-Western Railway (G&SWR), which developed the network further in Ayrshire and south-west Scotland, and served that area for seventy-three years until the grouping of the railways in 1923.

South from Ayr

By August 1840, the railway had opened throughout from Glasgow to Ayr, and straight away plans were made to extend the railway southwards to Ayr Harbour, and onwards to the seaside town of Girvan and the upland village of Dalmellington. Immediately, the Ayr and Galloway Railway was proposed to run from Ayr, via the Doon Valley, and over the hills to Castle Douglas to join the grandly named British and Irish Grand Junction Railway, which later opened as the Portpatrick Railway. This grand scheme never left the drawing board.

Corton, south of Ayr; LMS class 5MT '45147' 'Glasgow Highlander' (real no.45407) with 37405 heading for Stranraer (28 May 2000).

Dalrymple Junction; 37403 'Ben Cruachan' and 37408 'Loch Rannoch' Worksop Wanderer railtour (19 March 1994).

BELOW: *37428 crosses Burton Viaduct, Dalrymple with a railtour (13 August 2000).*
MAX FOWLER

Hollybush Station, closed 6 April 1964, now a private dwelling (1 August 2009).

However, circumstances changed in 1847. In that year, the Houldsworth family, industrialists from Manchester, opened an ironworks at Dunaskin, Waterside, and thus began the exploitation of the Doon Valley's mineral resources, a process that continued until very recently. From that year, loads of pig-iron began to stream down the road to Ayr Harbour for onward shipment. The newly formed Dalmellington Iron Company quickly expanded, the furnaces at Dunaskin consuming coal and iron ore mined from the surrounding hills. By 1850, the Company possessed several miles of railway and two steam locomotives, from Andrew Barclay's works in Kilmarnock, and Waterside had become a centre of great activity.

Hollybush; 37403 'Ben Cruachan' and 37408 'Loch Rannoch' 'Worksop Wanderer' (19 March 1994).

2 x class 37 hauled coal train from Chalmerston between Holehouse and Hollybush (March 1997). MAX FOWLER

Hollybush; 'Ayr Restorer' railtour 26028 and 26036 leading, with 37695 at the rear (13 July 1991).
CHARLES ROBINSON

All this had not escaped the attention of the local railway companies, which had amalgamated to form the Glasgow and South-Western Railway in 1850. A fresh proposal was put forward, more modestly titled 'The Ayr and Dalmellington Railway', which duly received parliamentary approval on 4 August 1853. To gain height from sea level in Ayr, up to the terminus in Dalmellington, the line took a fairly steeply graded and tortuous route via Dalrymple, through the villages of Hollybush (6¼ miles from Ayr), Patna (9¾) and Waterside (11¾) to the terminus at Dalmellington (15). The line was completed and opened for goods on 15 May 1856 and to passenger traffic on 7 August 1856.

EWSR 37405 at Polnessan with saloon, for the opening of the Broomhill opencast coal terminal (11 August 1998). MAX FOWLER

Mainline 60100 'Boar of Badenoch' at Waterside with a coal train from Chalmerston (c. 1994). ARCHIE THOM

Site of Waterside Station, looking north (26 September 2010).

The line south-west, to Maybole, was opened the following month, sharing the Dalmellington line to Dalrymple Junction, 3½ miles from Ayr. Stations were provided at Dalrymple (4 miles south of Ayr) and Cassillis (6), terminating at Maybole (10¼).

From Ayr, the Dalmellington trains worked from a temporary terminus at Townhead, until the new Ayr Station, at the same location, was completed on 1 July 1857, linking the line from Glasgow to the Dalmellington line, whereupon the temporary Townhead Station, and the original terminus from Glasgow at Ayr (Old) on North Harbour Street, closed to passengers but remained a goods depot for a further 115 years.

Railfreight Distribution 47289 passes Maybole with a Stranraer to Ayr 'Speedlink' train (6 July 1989).

Site of Kilkerran Station, closed 6 September 1965, looking south (15 November 2007).

With the opening of the railway south of the River Ayr to Ayr's new station in the centre of the town, and onwards to Dalmellington and Maybole, in 1856, eyes were cast southwards towards the fishing port of Girvan, the eventual goal being Stranraer and Portpatrick for the cross-channel traffic to Ireland. Construction started almost straight away on the remaining 12½ miles to Girvan, via the valley of the River Girvan. The line was quickly completed and opened on 24 May 1860, with stations located at Kilkerran (13¼ miles south of Ayr), Dailly (16), Killochan (18¾), terminating at Girvan (21¼). The line was double-track throughout, all the way from Ayr. It was to be another seventeen years before the railway was extended southwards to Stranraer.

BR 'Swindon' class 126 DMU at Killochan with a Stranraer to Glasgow Central train (10 May 1980). JIM DAVIDSON

GLASGOW AND SOUTH-WESTERN – THE NETWORK EVOLVES: 1850–80

BR 156509 calls at Girvan with the 11.23 Glasgow Central to Stranraer train (07 April 1995).

BELOW: First ScotRail 156447 awaits departure with the 19.10 Girvan to Kilmarnock train (14 September 2009).

LMS class 5MT 'Black 5's 44871 and 45407 at Girvan with the Great Britain III railtour, for Stranraer (10 April 2010).

There was one very short, goods-only branch, from the new line from Glengall Junction, about 3 miles south of Ayr, where a single-track swept steeply from the main line for half a mile to the Ailsa Psychiatric Hospital, mainly to bring coal in for the hospital's boilers. This was served by a trip working from Falkland Yard, Ayr, for decades. However, by November 1966 the branch had fallen into disuse, and the signal box was closed in November 1966.

Another separate company, the Girvan and Portpatrick Junction Railway, was formed to build the line onwards from Girvan to Stranraer. The distance along the coast is just over 30 miles, via the small fishing village of Ballantrae, but it is a rocky coastline, making the construction of a railway prohibitively expensive. Another route was explored, climbing away from Girvan to Barrhill, over bleak, largely unpopulated moorland, to join the recently completed railway (March 1861) from Dumfries to Stranraer, at Challoch, near the village of Dunragit. Due to difficulties in raising capital, authorization for the line was delayed and construction was not started until early in 1872. By early 1877, the line was largely complete and it duly opened for all traffic on 5 October 1877. The new railway left the existing line from Ayr to the north of Girvan Station, with a new station being provided to the south. The line was single-track throughout, with stations and passing loops provided at Pinmore (5¼ miles south of Girvan), Pinwherry (8¼), Barrhill (12¼), Glenwhilly (20¼) and New Luce (25), with a passing loop only provided at Challoch Junction (30½). At Challoch, there was a further 6½ miles to go over the existing railway from Dumfries before Stranraer was reached.

First ScotRail 156502 calls at Barrhill with the 19.12 Glasgow Central to Stranraer via Kilmarnock train (23 April 2010).

The new line was not an immediate success. Beset by financial troubles and setbacks, the situation was stabilized in 1892 when the Glasgow and South-Western Railway bought out the Girvan and Portpatrick Junction Railway.

Barrhead and Kilmarnock Joint Railway

By September 1848, the Glasgow, Barrhead and Neilston Railway (later to be absorbed by the Caledonian Railway) had reached the town of Barrhead, in Renfrewshire, 7½ miles south-west of Glasgow and only 16¼ miles from Kilmarnock. The rival Glasgow and South-Western Railway had proposals to reach Glasgow from Kilmarnock, and both companies prepared rival schemes for a railway to Kilmarnock, by the same route from Barrhead to Kilmarnock, more or less parallel to each other. Common sense prevailed in this instance (as it had between Glasgow and Paisley a few years earlier) and one single route was authorized, under the title of the Glasgow, Barrhead and Kilmarnock Joint Railway. The railway was built and opened to Stewarton, 11¼ miles from Barrhead, on 27 March 1871; the remaining 5½ miles to Kilmarnock open-

Kilmaurs up (southbound) side building prior to demolition (1971).
STUART RANKIN

Stewarton Station, looking north, before single-tracking and demolition of buildings (1971). STUART RANKIN

Dunlop Station, looking north, before single-tracking and demolition of buildings (1971). STUART RANKIN

ing on 26 June 1873, along with a 5-mile long branch from Lugton to Beith. There were thus two routes from Glasgow St Enoch to Kilmarnock, via Dalry (34½ miles) and now, more directly, via Barrhead (24¼ miles). Stations were provided at Neilston (2¼ miles from Barrhead), Caldwell (5¼), Lugton (7½), Dunlop (9¼), Stewarton (18¾) and Kilmaurs (23). Unlike the more circuitous route via Dalry, the Barrhead route was steeply graded, especially the 4½ miles between Barrhead and the summit at Shilford, a little north of Caldwell station. This resulted in slower times between Barrhead and Kilmarnock as trains battled with the steep gradients, taking as long as 15min to cover the 4½ miles. However, the Caledonian Railway had gained another foothold in Ayrshire at Kilmarnock.

This direct line eventually became an Anglo-Scottish main line (with the opening of the Midland Railway's Settle and Carlisle route) with the Glasgow and South-Western and Midland Railways operating jointly through express trains from Glasgow St Enoch to London St Pancras from May 1876.

ScotRail 156509 passes the site of Lugton Station (closed 7 November 1966) with a Glasgow Central to Kilmarnock train (12 July 1997).

The Ayrshire Lines

An important line was promoted and built eastwards from Ayr, through rich farming country, to Mauchline, linking the line from Glasgow to Ayr with the main line from Glasgow to Carlisle via Kilmarnock and Dumfries. This left the main Glasgow line 1¼ miles north of the new Ayr Station at Hawkhill Junction and immediately struck eastwards for 10¼ miles to Mauchline, where the main line to Dumfries and Carlisle was joined. At Newton-on-Ayr, a chord was built to enable trains to run onto the Mauchline line from the north, from Newton Junction to Blackhouse Junction. Within this triangle, Ayr engine sheds were established in 1879, replacing the small shed adjacent to the old passenger terminus on the north bank of the River Ayr.

The Ayr to Mauchline, which was double-track throughout, was opened on 1 September 1870; stations were provided at Auchicruive (3 miles from Ayr), Annbank (actually in the village of Mossblown, a mile from Annbank) (5 miles) and Tarbolton (a mile and a half from the village) (7 miles from Ayr).

The next new line was the 'A&C' (Ayr and Cumnock) cross-country railway, linking Ayr and Cumnock, and eventually the mining village of Muirkirk. This largely single-line branch ran from

Hawkhill Junction, Ayr; BR class 27 D5347 and a BR 'Standard 5' pass with the Newcastle to Stranraer train (c. 1963). BILL HAMILTON

BR 27027 heads an engineers' train up the Mauchline line at Heathfield, Ayr on 18 May 1977. ARTHUR WILSON

LMS class 5MT 'Black 5' 44785 with a southbound goods train heads up the Mauchline line at Heathfield, Ayr (early 1960s).
BILL HAMILTON

BR Trainload Coal 56124 passes the site of Mossblown Junction with empty coal hopper wagons from Killoch (9 July 1993).

Annbank Junction, with its lofty signal box, shortly before closure and demolition (17 March 1985). ARTHUR WILSON

BR Trainload Coal 37693 and 37071 at Annbank Junction with a coal train from Killoch (March 1993). MAX FOWLER

LNER K4 class 61994 'The Great Marquess' approaches Tarbolton with the 07.48 Barnhill (Glasgow) to Carlisle railtour (22 September 2014).

LMS class 5MT 'Black 5' 45160 passes Tarbolton Station, closed 4 January 1943 (early 1960s). BILL HAMILTON

BR Trainload Coal 37139 and 37377 between Annbank and Trabboch with coal from Chalmerston to Killoch for blending (11 June 1992).

Annbank Junction, 5 miles east of Ayr, on the Ayr to Mauchline line across the Ayrshire countryside to the small industrial town of Muirkirk, which already had a branch line from Auchinleck, on the main line from Kilmarnock to Dumfries. At 27¾ miles long, it passed close to several settlements and villages, but the only real centre of population it passed through was Cumnock, also on the Kilmarnock–Dumfries line. The railway was completed and opened for goods traffic on 11 June 1872, and for passengers shortly after, on 1 July. At the end of that year, a connecting line, 6 miles long, was opened between Belston Junction, 6 miles from Annbank Junction, to Holehouse Junction on the Dalmellington branch. From Annbank Junction, stations were provided at (distances in miles from Ayr) Trabboch (7¾), Drongan (9¾, opened on 8 March 1876), Ochiltree (14¼), Skares (15¼), Dumfries House (16), Cumnock (18¼) and Cronberry (21¼) terminating

BR 37217 and 37139 crossing Enterkine Viaduct over the River Ayr with loaded coal hoppers for Killoch (30 October 1991).
ARTHUR WILSON

BR 37116 and 37212 pass the site of Drongan Station, closed 10 September 1951, with empty coal hoppers from Killoch (26 August 1994).

BR 37111 'Glengarnock' and 37080 near the site of Trabboch Station, closed 10 September 1951, with loaded coal hoppers for Killoch (8 July 1994).

with an end-on junction with the Caledonian Railway at Muirkirk Station (27). An end-on junction occurs where two railways meet end to end, forming a continuous railway line (as at Muirkirk in the station). The line was single-track from Annbank Junction to Muirkirk, with passing loops at some stations. Trains were generally allowed an hour to cover the 27 miles from Ayr to Muirkirk.

Signal boxes were provided at Drumdow, Drongan, Belston Junction (line to Rankinston and Holehouse Junction), Burnockhill (branch to Burnockhill Pit), Ochiltree, Dykes Junction (line to Whitehill and Hindsward Pits), Dumfries House, Cumnock, Logan Junction (spur to Kilmarnock–Dumfries line), Cronberry Junction (line to Auchinleck), Gass Water Junction (branch to Cairn Pit), Stonebriggs

Site of Ochiltree Station, closed 10 September 1951, now a private dwelling (1 May 2008).

Site of Skares Station, closed 10 September 1951, now occupied by a modern private dwelling (1 May 2008).

and Muirkirk. The various collieries, or 'pits', all provided steady traffic for the line. At Muirkirk, the Glasgow and South-Western made an end-on junction with the Caledonian Railway, and shared the same two-platform through station (i.e. not a terminus), which was originally opened in 1848 when the branch from Auchinleck was opened.

The passenger service was always very sparse, with a maximum of five trains a day (extras on Saturdays) being provided over the whole length of the line during its lifetime; taking just under an hour for the journey from Muirkirk to Ayr. As soon as the line opened, there were demands for a direct service to Edinburgh via Murkirk and Lanark; one return working per day was provided. (A return working is where a train works from one place to another, and returns using the same route to its original starting point.) However, the service was poorly patronized, it still being quicker and costing no more to travel to Glasgow and across to Edinburgh via the North British Railway from Queen Street or the Caledonian Railway from Glasgow Central.

East of Muirkirk, the Caledonian Railway's line linked Muirkirk with Lanark, the railway leaving Ayrshire at Glenbuck, 4 miles east of Muirkirk. However, always keen to compete for traffic with the G&SWR, the Caledonian Railway (CR) promoted and built another railway from its Lanarkshire heartland in an attempt to take advantage of the booming coal and iron traffic that Muirkirk generated – a railway that was built but never opened. The CR obtained authorization to build their Mid-Lanarkshire Lines extension, linking Strathaven and Stonehouse with Muirkirk, to counter the G&SWR incursion into Lanarkshire, and to tap into the lucrative mineral traffic originating in Muirkirk. The CR's line northwards started at Auldhouseburn Junction, immediately east of Muirkirk Station, crossed over the River Ayr on a large viaduct, then headed across bleak moorland, over the Ponesk Burn and Stottencleaugh Burn on further expensive viaducts, to the remote Spyreslack Colliery, and onwards, north-east, linking with the existing railway at Coalburn, a total of some 8 miles. The line was completed, and fully signalled, but only the portion from Coalburn to Spyreslack was ever opened for traffic. The section onwards to Muirkirk never, ever saw a revenue-earning train; it was said that this was to prevent the G&SWR from exercising running powers over the line, which was eventually lifted and dismantled in the 1920s.

Muirkirk's industrial prosperity peaked during the early years of the twentieth century, but following the First World War, and with the closure of the iron furnaces in 1923, the fortunes of the railway started to decline.

West Kilbride; 318022 calling with the 15.45 Glasgow Central–Largs (10 September 2007).

First ScotRail 380112 departs from Fairlie with the 07.15 Glasgow Central to Largs train (20 April 2012).

The seaside towns of Seamill and the adjoining West Kilbride, Fairlie and Largs, had always provided an attraction to the railway promoters. In 1840, the railway had reached Ardrossan and the logical step was to extend the line northwards along the coast. A number of years passed before this became a reality. The distance from Ardrossan to Largs was only 11¾ miles, but the line was built in stages. The first section, 4¾ miles, was opened on 1 May 1878, followed on 1 June 1880 to Fairlie (9¼ miles) and finally, on 1 June 1885, to the terminus at Largs. On 1 June 1882, a very short branch was opened to the new Fairlie Pier from Fairlie Pier Junction; a connection with steamers to Brodick on the Isle of Arran was established from that date, with boat trains running direct from Glasgow St Enoch.

First ScotRail 334036 passes Fairlie Pier Junction, and approaches Fairlie Tunnel with the 08.38 Largs to Glasgow Central train (28 August 2009).

ABOVE: BR 20002 and 20122 at Largs with an excursion train from Liverpool (June 1977).
ARTHUR WILSON

LEFT: Panoramic view of Largs; BR 40065 plus several DMUs (c. 1971).
BILL HAMILTON

The effect of electrification and rationalization at Largs; BR 318269 leaves with the 15.50 to Glasgow Central (15 August 1987).

With the formation of the Glasgow and South-Western Railway in 1850, a substantial amount of new railway had been built relatively quickly. The new railway required locomotives, passenger carriages and goods wagons of different kinds. All these items were acquired, and the various passenger and goods services were introduced and developed. The company's locomotive works were established in Kilmarnock, and they were responsible for the overhauling of the locomotive stud. The works were situated in the triangle between the line to Troon and the line to Dalry, just north of Kilmarnock Station. They were opened in 1856, replacing a much smaller facility at Cook Street in Glasgow. Construction and maintenance of carriages and wagons were also undertaken in Kilmarnock.

Principal engine sheds were established at Muirkirk, Kilmarnock, Ayr and Ardrossan, as well as outside Ayrshire at Greenock, Corkerhill (Glasgow) and Currock (Carlisle), and many smaller sheds. All were eventually expanded and relocated, as we shall see in subsequent chapters.

The Caledonian Railway

Right through this period, the Glasgow and South-Western Railway totally dominated the region. All lines were built and operated by the G&SWR. This was not universally accepted with delight by the towns and villages served by the new railways; in particular, the traders of Ayr and, to a lesser extent, Kilmarnock, saw this as a monopoly and felt they were being held to ransom as regards the rates charged for the carriage of goods. It was widely felt that some competition was needed, and when the G&SWR's arch rival, the Caledonian Railway, showed an interest in extending their railway from Cathcart in Glasgow, all the way to the port of Ardrossan, various parties in Ayrshire showed willing support.

Since May 1873, the CR had access to Kilmarnock, Ayrshire's main industrial centre, with the opening of the Glasgow, Barrhead and Kilmarnock Joint Railway. However, a railway exclusive to the Caledonian was the ultimate objective. A new line was proposed, from Barrmill on the Joint line's branch from Lugton to Beith, to Kilwinning, a distance of 6 miles; it was subsequently extended on to Ardrossan Harbour, another 6 miles, with a 4-mile branch from Giffen, 2 miles south of Barrmill to the iron- and steel-producing town of Kilbirnie. These proposals were approved by Parliament, and the Barrmill to Ardrossan Railway was opened in September 1888, with the branch to Kilbirnie opening some fifteen months later. The extension to Ardrossan Montgomerie Pier and the branch from Kilwinning to Irvine opened simultaneously in June 1890. Thus the CR had its own route to Ardrossan, and could compete for the lucrative ferry traffic to Arran and coal exports from Ardrossan.

However, on the Glasgow to Lugton and Barrmill section, the CR had to share track with the G&SWR, which was far from ideal. Further developments on the south side of Glasgow by the CR led to the creation of the 'Cathcart Circle', which, of course, is still with us today. At Cathcart, the railway was not far from Barrhead and, a few miles further southwest, Lugton. Thus, a new line was proposed from Newton, on the CR's main Glasgow to Carlisle line, through the area to the south-east of Glasgow, to Cathcart, and onwards to Neilston near Barrhead, and 9 miles onwards to Giffen via Lugton. This would give the CR a completely independent route from Glasgow to Ayrshire.

This new line, the 'Lanarkshire and Ayrshire' duly received parliamentary approval in July 1897, and was completed within a few years. The line from Cathcart to Barrmill (linking with the existing line to Ardrossan) opened at the beginning of June 1903. The link eastwards from Cathcart to Newton followed in January 1906. South of Cathcart, stations were provided at Muirend, Whitecraigs, Patterton, Neilston (all in Renfrewshire and all still open today), thereafter at Uplawmoor, Lugton High, Giffen, Auchenmade, Kilwinning East, Stevenston Moorpark, Saltcoats North, Ardrossan North and the terminus at Ardrossan Montgomerie Pier. The total distance from Glasgow Central to Ardrossan by the CR route was 31½ miles, compared with the G&SWR's from St Enoch to Ardrossan of 32¼.

A branch line 3 miles long, was built from Kilwinning East to the next town down the coast, Irvine. The branch was built single-track, with one intermediate halt at Bogside. There was a good-sized terminus provided at Bank Street in Irvine. This had the advantage of being in the town centre, as opposed to the G&SWR's station, which was located further away to the west, towards the harbour.

Initially, the passenger train service was good, with a dozen trains between Glasgow Central and Ardrossan, including boat trains. The branch to Irvine was well served also, with thirteen trains each way on weekdays, and an extra return working on Saturdays. However, the 'Caley' line never rivalled the long-established Glasgow and South-Western line, and after the grouping of the railways in 1923, which brought both routes to Ardrossan under the control of one company, the writing was on the wall for the 'Lanarkshire and Ayrshire'.

From Kilwinning, the aim of the Caledonian Railway was to extend their line by 12¼ miles from Kilwinning, via Irvine, Troon and Prestwick, to Ayr, effectively duplicating the G&SWR's line. This received the widespread support of the business community in Ayrshire, disenchanted with the G&SWR's near monopoly in Ayr. A scheme was drawn up, doubling the Irvine branch and extending the line to Ayr. A branch to Troon Harbour was included, with connections to the G&SWR's Ayr to Mauchline line, so the CR would have running powers to Muirkirk. Maybe fortuitously, this scheme never came to fruition, due in part to the G&SWR's strong opposition, thereby avoiding an expensive duplication of railways in Ayrshire.

That was the extent of the 'enemy' Caledonian Railway's incursion into Ayrshire. The 'dominant force', the Glasgow and South-Western Railway, continued to expand. After the opening of the two main lines (Glasgow to Ayr, and Glasgow to Kilmarnock, Dumfries and Carlisle), extensions of the network were pursued.

Engineering Landmarks

Despite the diverse terrain that the various lines of the Glasgow and South-Western Railway (and its constituent companies) passed through, there were a few notable structures and heavy works undertaken worthy of mention, many of which still carrying main-line traffic today.

On the Kilmarnock to Dumfries section, there is the 23-arch masonry viaduct immediately to the south of Kilmarnock Station, 60ft (18.5m) high. Between Kilmarnock and Mauchline is Mossgiel

Ballochmyle Viaduct spanning the River Ayr gorge (June 1966).
THOMAS McMILLAN

Tunnel, 2,050ft (625m) long. This is the longest tunnel in Ayrshire.

A mile south of Mauchline is the major railway structure in Ayrshire, the Ballochmyle Viaduct. This magnificent sandstone viaduct carries the Kilmarnock–Dumfries–Carlisle main line over a gorge of the River Ayr. It has seven spans in total, three 50ft (15m) spans either side of the main central span of 181ft (55m). The crown of the large central arch is 163ft (50m) above the River Ayr.

A few miles further south again, just north of Cumnock, is the Templand Viaduct (Lugar Water Viaduct), over the valley of the Lugar Water. It has fourteen arches, and is 145ft (44m) above the river. The Glaisnock Viaduct is also in Cumnock, on the Cumnock to Muirkirk line (closed in 1962). It has thirteen arches and the highest is 75ft (23m); the viaduct is 1,706ft (520m) long, and has been laid out as a footpath linking two areas of the town.

On the Dalmellington branch, the Burnton

Templand Viaduct, Cumnock (20 January 2011).

Dykes Viaduct, Skares (1 May 2008).

Stewarton (Annick Water) Viaduct (8 September 2010).

Viaduct, close to the village of Dalrymple, is noteworthy. This is a substantial stone structure of sixteen arches with a maximum height of 83ft (25m).

On the Ayr and Cumnock line, between Annbank Junction and Cumnock, there are two noteworthy viaducts. The first is at Enterkine, south of Annbank, carrying the single-track (but built optimistically for double-track), over the River Ayr. Twelve stone piers carry the line over the valley and river, topped by a steel deck. At its greatest height it is 108ft (33m) above the river. This is unlike the other viaducts in the area, which are of masonry arches.

Further east, between Ochiltree and Skares, was Burnockhill Viaduct, a major structure of twelve arches. A few miles further on is Skares, or Dykes Viaduct, similar to Burnockhill but half the length.

Beyond Cumnock Station is located the Glaisnock Viaduct. This is 525ft (160m) long, and at its greatest height is 75ft (23m) high. The railway over it closed in July 1964 and there is now a public footpath along it.

The spectacular Annick Water Viaduct dominates the southern approaches to Stewarton, on the Glasgow, Barrhead and Kilmarnock Joint Railway. The railway is still open; in fact double-track was

Rankinston Viaduct (2 August 2010).

Gree Viaduct, near Lugton, before demolition (14 August 2003).

reinstated over it in 2009 as part of the upgrading of the Glasgow to Kilmarnock line. There was an unfortunate incident in April 2010 when an engineer died whilst inspecting the viaduct from a cherrypicker, the machine toppling over and the man drowning in the river below.

There are two masonry viaducts near Rankinston on the Belston Junction to Holehouse Junction line. Both still exist and are well maintained, and fenced off. They were in use until late 1974, carrying coal trains from the nearby Littlemill Colliery.

The Gree Viaduct, near Lugton, was an impressive eleven-arch structure, carrying the Caledonian's Lanarkshire and Ayrshire Railway's line to Ardrossan over the Lugton Water. It survived the closure of the line by fifty years, but was demolished in 2007 due to its unsafe condition.

The seven-arch Garnock Viaduct, on the northern outskirts of Kilwinning, took the Caledonian's line to Ardrossan over the River Garnock. It survives to this day, carrying a footpath and cycleway. A street nearby is named 'Viaduct Crescent'.

Garnock Viaduct, Kilwinning (27 August 2007).

CHAPTER 3

Later Additions: 1880–1923

By 1880, with the basic network complete and established, the Glasgow and South-Western Railway embarked upon improvements and further new lines. Traffic, both goods and passenger, was developing nicely, and the 'Sou'west' was an ambitious railway.

With the opening of the west to east Ayr and Cumnock Railway (A&C) in 1872, the opportunity was taken to link it to the nearby Dalmellington branch, giving Dalmellington and the ironworks at Waterside a direct link with the south via Cumnock.

A new line was surveyed between its nearest points, from Holehouse Junction, between Hollybush and Patna on the Dalmellington line, to Belston Junction between Drongan and Ochiltree on the A&C, a total length of a little under 6 miles. It was opened purely as a goods-only railway, serving several coal and ironstone mines along its length. A small village was established at Rankinston to house the workers nearby, and a passenger station was opened there on 1 January 1884. The line was served initially by a Dalmellington–Muirkirk passenger service, but

Re-laying Holehouse Junction (June 1998).
ARCHIE THOM

Broomhill (August 1998). ARCHIE THOM

this was not used to any extent and the service was cut back to six return Dalmellington to Rankinston trips. Passengers from Rankinston to Ayr had to change at the exchange platform at Holehouse Junction (provided from 1901) or 1¼ miles further on at Patna. Towards the end of passenger services on the line, there was a curious working. A Dalmellington to Ayr train worked via Rankinston, and on to Belston Junction, where it reversed and proceeded to Ayr via Drongan and Annbank.

In 1901, an exchange platform was built at Holehouse Junction, where connections to Dalmellington–Ayr trains were made. There was no public access to the platform at Holehouse. By 1913, there were six arrivals/departures at Rankinston.

The ironstone pits were worked out by the start of the First World War, but coal-mining kept the community at Rankinston, and its railway, going. Large mines were developed at nearby Polquhairn and Littlemill, and the country's appetite for coal meant that mining continued to thrive until the 1960s.

The seaside town, and port, of Troon, in common with most other towns, grew with the coming of the railway to Glasgow in 1840. The branch to the harbour was very busy, mostly with the export of coal; all traffic had to come via Barassie, to the north of the town. In the early 1890s, the Troon Loop Line was built, improving connections to Troon Harbour by creating rail access for traffic from the Ayr direction, with the bonus of providing a new passenger station much closer to the town centre. This new line left the main line immediately south of Barassie Station, and rejoined the main line at Lochgreen Junction, 2 miles south of Barassie. A spur left this line at Troon Junction, just south of the new Troon Station, on an embankment through the town, to the harbour, joining the existing line from Barassie at Templehill. The central part of the new loop line was built on an embankment to save several level-crossings in the town centre. The new line and station was opened on 2 May 1892, while the existing passenger station on the direct line closed on that date and became goods-only.

BR 26043 arrives at Barassie Junction with an engineers' train; Troon loop bears off to the right (26 June 1987).

Troon; DB Schenker 66154 heads south with a coal train whilst a Freightliner heavy haul coal train waits in the loop for access to the Kilmarnock branch (30 September 2010).

Troon (new station); LNER design class A1 60163 'Tornado' passes with the 10.08 Carlisle–Carlisle 'Border Reiver' (27 June 2015).

BR 47108 departs Troon with Sealink stock on the 11.35 Glasgow Central to Stranraer (5 April 1985).
ARTHUR WILSON

BELOW: BR Transrail 37221 passes the site of Lochgreen Junction and heads onto the Troon loop line (10 April 1998).

Freightliner 66529 passes the site of Lochgreen Junction with a southbound coal train (16 June 2010).

LATER ADDITIONS: 1880–1923

ABOVE: *Colas Railfreight 56105 approaches the site of Lochgreen Junction with Prestwick Airport to Grangemouth empty aviation fuel tankers (20 September 2013).*

Unidentified Caledonian Railway 'Jumbo' at Troon Harbour (late 1950s). BILL HAMILTON

It was at Barassie Junction on 4 February 1898 that the worst train accident in Ayrshire occurred, when an early morning goods train from Ayr to Glasgow, heading north on the direct line, collided with the 7.00am passenger and mail train from Kilmarnock to Ayr at the junction. The signalman at Barassie Junction had set his signals for the mail train to run off the Kilmarnock line and onto the new loop, to make its booked stop at Troon. The goods train was obliged to stop at the signal protecting the junction, but it didn't, and collided with the mail train. This, however, was not the correct method of regulating the two trains in such a situation. The Glasgow-bound goods train should have had the right of way, with the points set for the Kilmarnock train to go down the direct line if it overshot its signals at danger. So why, if the signals were at danger on the direct line, did the goods train not stop? The enquiry found that the distant signal, to the south of Barassie Junction, was not distinctly showing the danger position, and the driver of the goods train interpreted it as clear, not caution, which would have indicated that the next (home) signal was at danger (which indeed it was). By the time he saw the home signal at danger, it was too late to stop and the collision occurred. Altogether, seven people were killed at what became known as 'the Barassie Disaster'.

In connection with the improved access to Troon Harbour from the south, a double-track spur some 2½ miles long was opened from Mossblown Junction, west of Annbank Junction, east of Ayr, to Monkton, north of Prestwick. This enabled trains from the lines east of Ayr to bypass Ayr entirely. Save for periodic passenger diversions, this line saw only goods traffic.

The railway up the Irvine valley, east of Kilmarnock through Galston to Newmilns, was at last extended to Darvel, opening for all traffic on 1 June 1886. From leaving the Kilmarnock to Dumfries line at Hurlford Junction, the distance to Darvel was 7½ miles. By 1923, there were eleven trains each way, with two extra on Saturdays.

This railway was extended to Strathaven, 11 miles to the east in Lanarkshire. Strathaven, part of the Caledonian Railway empire, was already connected to Glasgow via Hamilton. The logical step seemed to be to connect the town with Darvel, providing an additional and potentially useful east-to-west route avoiding the busy Lanarkshire–Glasgow network of lines. The Glasgow and South-Western and the Caledonian Railways jointly built the line and it opened for all traffic on 1 May 1905. There were two stations, at Loudounhill (2¾ miles from Darvel) and, over the border in Lanarkshire, at Drumclog

BR track-recording train on the Riccarton branch, Kilmarnock (31 July 1991).

DRS 37601 at the tail of the 'Galloway Galloper' railtour visiting the Riccarton branch, Kilmarnock (12 February 2011).

(5½) and Ryeland (7¼). The line was worked every alternate six months by the two rival companies. The line gave the Lanarkshire coalfields direct access to the Ayrshire ports.

Kilmarnock, with five lines converging on it, along with the locomotive works, engine shed and a busy passenger station, was becoming very congested, so a 'bypass' line was planned to the south of the town. Leaving the Irvine Valley line from Darvel at Mayfield Junction, east of Hurlford Mineral Sidings, it ran through Riccarton on the south side of Kilmarnock, then met the Kilmarnock and Troon line at Thirdpart Junction, a short distance east of Gatehead Station. The length of the new line was just over 4 miles. The double-track line was opened on 14 July 1902, with a station provided at Riccarton and Cragie, halfway along the line. However, this was never opened to a regular passenger service, being used only for special excursions. The line fulfilled its purpose of relieving congestion through Kilmarnock Station, and had regular goods trains passing along it; there was a busy goods station at Riccarton. Kilmarnock Power station was established adjacent to the line at Riccarton, taking trainloads of coal up to its closure in 1970.

A short length of line was opened on 6 June 1904, linking Bellfield Junction on the Hurlford–Gatehead line just east of Riccarton, to Kay Park Junction on the main line, a mile south of Kilmarnock Station. This enabled trains passing south through Kilmarnock to turn to the west and to the Glasgow to Ayr line via the Kilmarnock and Troon line. This was invaluable as a diversionary route if the Glasgow to Ayr line was blocked.

The branch line to the village of Catrine was a later addition to the G&SWR system. Catrine is a village of some 1,200 inhabitants, on the river Ayr 14 miles south-east of Kilmarnock and 2 miles from

LMS 'Fairburn' class 4MT 42277 comes up the Catrine branch with a railtour (20 June 1962). BILL HAMILTON

RIGHT: The Catrine branch, forty-five years after closure (12 October 2009).

BELOW: *Postcard of Catrine Station.*
TERRY HARRISON COLLECTION

Mauchline on the G&SW's main line from Kilmarnock to Dumfries and Carlisle. It was served by the station at Mauchline but, in 1898, the G&SWR decided to build a branch line to serve the village and its mill. The necessary powers were obtained, the branch and station at Catrine built (there were no intermediate stations) and the line was opened for business on 1 September 1903.

The new branch left the Kilmarnock–Dumfries line 2 miles south of Mauchline at Brackenhill junction, and descended the 1½ miles from the Junction to the terminus situated to the west of St Germain Street in Catrine, beside the bridge over the River Ayr. The branch was single-track throughout, and worked by the 'one engine in steam' principle. It was very steeply graded, the difference in height from the junction to the terminus about 52m (160ft), an average gradient of 1 in 60.

The branch led a relatively quiet existence, there generally being four trains a day from Catrine to Mauchline, where connections to Kilmarnock, Glasgow, Dumfries and Ayr were provided, with two extras on Saturdays. Generally, one or two coaches sufficed for the traffic, hauled by elderly tank engines. However, for a few years, a Manson steam railmotor was used successfully; it was known as the 'Catrine Caur'. Three were built by the G&SWR and no.1 was the regular at Catrine. During the early years of the Second World War, some 'foreign' locomotives were brought to Ayr, and it is reported that a London and South-Western Railway 0-4-2 tank engine, on loan from the Southern Railway, was used for periods on the Catrine branch. The textile mill in the village kept the small goods yard busy, with the finished product leaving Catrine by rail, as well as raw materials and other general supplies, e.g. coal and agricultural items, arriving.

As always with quiet branch lines, after the grouping in 1923, better roads and the growth of bus services had an adverse impact on passenger numbers at Catrine. There was a temporary closure during the First World War, but on 3 May 1943 passenger services ceased for good. The service by this time had been extended to Ayr via Mauchline and Annbank Junction, so at that time the intermediate station of Tarbolton also closed. However, goods traffic and the occasional passenger special still ran, the goods yard being served by a daily train from Ayr.

Occasional passenger excursions were made by local working mens' clubs (a sizable proportion of Catrine's working population was employed in the local coal-mines) and Sunday School trips to the seaside at Girvan, Ayr, Prestwick and Troon. Any enthusiast railtours that came to the area always

Postcard of Catrine Station.
TERRY HARRISON COLLECTION

Postcard of Catrine Station.
TERRY HARRISON

had a trip down the branch. LMS 2P no.40574 visited on 9 May 1959, and LMS class 4MT no.42277 was noted on 20 June 1962. The daily goods train was latterly worked by any Ayr-based locomotive: LMS 'Black 5s', Fowler 'Crabs' and even an LNER class B1.

The decline of the textile mill in Catrine, with the growth of road transport, hastened the end of the little branch, and British Railways (rebranded 'British Rail' in 1965) closed the line entirely on 6 July 1964, with the signal box on the main line at Brackenhill Junction following on. The track was removed within a year.

Very little trace of the line or the station can be found in Catrine now. The site is a small industrial estate, but earthworks and a couple of overbridges (including the main A76 Kilmarnock–Dumfries road overbridge) can still be seen.

The long-established main lines from Glasgow to Paisley, and south-west to the Ayrshire coastal towns, together with the branch from Dalry to Kilmarnock, and thence south to Dumfries and Carlisle, had become very heavily used; the Glasgow & South-Western looked at ways to relieve the congestion. The answer lay in the last great railway project of the era – the Lochwinnoch loop line (or the Dalry and North Johnstone line). The new railway left the Paisley to Greenock line at Cart Junction west of Elderslie, and struck south-westwards, parallel to the Ayr line, which it rejoined at Brownhill Junction, just north of Dalry, the total distance being slightly under 14 miles. The course of the new line was to the north-west of, and never more than a mile from, the Paisley to Ayr line. New stations were provided at Johnstone North, Kilbarchan, Lochwinnoch (in Renfrewshire) and Kilbirnie.

The last railway to be built in Ayrshire was the the Maidens and Dunure Light Railway, including the luxury (and still world-famous) Turnberry Hotel and golf courses. Ayr and Girvan had been linked by the railway since 1860, with the route ignoring the coast and passing inland via Maybole and the valley of the River Girvan. The Glasgow and South-Western Railway saw the potential of a coastal route between the two towns, which were 2 miles apart, bringing the small fishing communities of Dunure and Maidens, as well as the Culzean Castle and Estate, into the railway network. Authorization was duly granted, and construction started. Concurrently, the Glasgow and South-Western Railway commissioned the design of a massive luxury hotel and championship-standard links golf course at the seaside village of

River Doon Viaduct, Alloway (18 March 2008).

Alloway Tunnel (18 March 2008).

BELOW: **Heads of Ayr, showing the course of the Maidens and Dunure Light Railway** *(31 July 2005).*

Site of Dunure Station, closed 1 December 1930 (6 April 2009).

Overbridge to the south of Glenside Station (2 June 2013).

Turnberry, on the coast 2 miles south of Maidens. This was intended, and succeeded, in matching a similar development by the Caledonian Railway, at Gleneagles in Perthshire, on the main line between Glasgow and Perth.

The hotel, golf courses and railway were completed and the entire enterprise was opened with great publicity on 17 May 1906. The new railway was single-track throughout, with passing loops at the stations. It left the existing line south of Ayr at Alloway Junction, 1¾ miles south of Ayr, rejoining it ¾ mile north of Girvan station, a total distance of 19¾ miles. Stations were provided at Alloway (3 miles from Ayr), Greenan Castle (goods only), Heads of Ayr (6¼), Dunure (8), Balchriston (goods only), Knoweside (11), Glenside (13), Maidens (15¼), Turnberry (16¾ miles), and Dipple (goods only). Subsequent to the line opening, a halt was opened at Balchriston level-crossing, to serve a few surrounding farms. Just prior to the outbreak of the Second World War, an ordnance factory was opened at Grangeston, 1½ miles north of Girvan, which was served by sidings on the Turnberry line. A halt was provided for the workers, but this was situated on the inland route, on the other side of the factory. The station at Glenside served Culzean Castle half a mile away; the station even had a private waiting room for the Marquis of Ailsa.

BELOW: *Turnberry Hotel (21 September 2013).*

Glasgow and South-Western Railway timetable on display at Turnberry Golf Club (21 September 2013).

between the main line to Dumfries and Carlisle, and the branch to Darvel. Hurlford Mineral Sidings, to handle traffic from the coal-mines in the vicinity, was also established here, and two rows of terraced houses, to the latest standards, were built for the Company's employees. A halt on the Darvel branch was provided, called 'Barlieth', but not until 1927. The new complex was opened in 1877, with a centralized stores building added a few years later.

The old shed in Kilmarnock was not abandoned but continued to coal, water and service locomotives until around 1960. Latterly, the building survived as part of the Johnnie Walker whisky complex, and was not demolished until 2013.

The Maidens and Dunure Light Railway had a passenger service of six trains each way, Mondays to Saturdays, with no service on Sundays. However, Turnberry Hotel enjoyed through coaches from Glasgow St Enoch, and for a long period, a through sleeping coach from London Euston. Turnberry Station was situated opposite the main entrance to the hotel, and was directly linked by a covered walkway. The hotel and golf courses were an instant success, and contributed greatly to the early success of the line.

During this period, the facilities that the Glasgow and South-Western Railway had developed at Kilmarnock were being outgrown by the number of new railways growing around them. The locomotive shed at Kilmarnock, established in 1843, adjacent to the station on the north side, had become inadequate, so the Company decided in 1873 to supersede the facilities with a new, purpose-built, modern depot at Hurlford, 2 miles south of Kilmarnock. The new locomotive shed was built on land

LMS class 5MT 'Black 5' 45192 at Hurlford shed, the 'blocks' (housing) in the background (early 1960s). BILL HAMILTON

Caledonian Railway class 3F 57650 at Hurlford shed (late 1950s). BILL HAMILTON

LMS class 5MT 'Black 5' 44962 (?) passes Hurlford Shed with a southbound goods train (late 1950s). BILL HAMILTON

Irvine; 08693, 20048 and 20063 stabled, S&T works in the background (3 August 1986).

Barassie looking south; the site of the wagon works is in the background (1 March 2012).

The by now inadequate and outdated facilities for carriage and wagon construction and repairs at Kilmarnock were also relocated. A new carriage and wagon works was built at Barassie, in the fork of the Troon direct line and loop line, just south of Barassie Station and the junction of the Glasgow and Kilmarnock lines; the new workshops were opened in 1901. Modernized by British Rail as recently as 1965, Barassie Works closed in 1971. Signalling and telegraphics (S&T) were catered for at purpose-built workshops at Irvine, immediately to the east of the Paisley–Glasgow main line, just south of Irvine Station. The workshops survived in use until 1986, when modernization and electrification rendered them redundant.

The S&T workshops at Irvine and the carriage and wagon works at Barassie occupied condiderable areas of land, and upon closure of the railway facilities, became ripe for redevelopment. The Irvine site is now part of the Riverway Retail Park; at Barassie, part of the site is given over to housing, while most of it was used as a depot for the mid-1980s electrification work on the Ayr to Glasgow line, and is still rail-connected but now derelict.

CHAPTER 4

The London, Midland and Scottish Railway (LMS) Era: 1923–48

The effort of Britain (and its allies) in waging and emerging victorious in the 'Great War' 1914–18 left the country drained. A good proportion of the male population had been lost in the conflict, and those that survived must have come home mentally and physically exhausted. There were many celebrations at the cessation of hostilities, but there must have been a huge sense of relief also.

Industry had made a huge effort to manufacture weapons, munitions, aircraft, warships and equipment of all kinds to enable the armed forces to wage a successful campaign, while the railways were stretched to capacity to transfer men and equipment all over the country. At the time of the First World War, all of Ireland was part of Great Britain, so the port of Stranraer was a very busy facility linking Ireland with the northern part of Britain. During the conflict, traffic to and from Ireland from Scotland's central belt travelled south through Ayrshire. The Glasgow and South-Western Railway was no exception in being worked to the limit with wartime traffic, so much so that locomotives and rolling stock were borrowed, where possible, from other railways.

After the Great War, the government of the day saw that action was necessary to breathe new life (and investment) into the railways, which, of course, at the time were the principal means of transport in Britain. The answer was to amalgamate over 150 independent companies throughout Britain into four large companies, based on their geographical locations.

The Railways Act was passed on 19 August 1921, and the Glasgow and South-Western Railway was to become part of the London, Midland and Scottish Railway, in common with its neighbour and competitor, the Caledonian Railway, and, further north, The Highland Railway.

After over seventy-two years in existence, during which time it developed most of the railways in the Glasgow/Carlisle/Stranraer region, the Glasgow and South-Western Railway ceased to exist on 1 January 1923. The G&SWR became part of the London, Midland and Scottish Railway (LMS), one of only two of the post-grouping companies in Scotland (the London and North Eastern Railway was the other). The first few years made little difference to what went before. Locomotives were renumbered and a new livery was introduced – maroon replacing green for passenger locomotives, goods locos remaining black. Gradually G&SWR signs and notices were replaced with LMS versions. These changes were cosmetic, but in the light of economies, which were becoming necessary due to the worsening economic climate in Britain generally, together with the growth of motorized road transport, drastic changes were needed; this meant something hitherto unknown on the railways – closures.

Early Economies

Almost immediately, the LMS had a look at their two main lines from Glasgow into Ayrshire: the ex-G&SWR route via Paisley and Kilwinning to Ayr (including the Lochwinnoch loop), with the branch to the ports of Ardrossan and Largs; and the rather more direct route from Glasgow via Cathcart, Neilston and Kilwinning to Ardrossan, with the branches to Kilbirnie and Irvine.

When the LMS took over the Caledonian Railway's main line to Ardrossan (Montgomerie Pier), there were eight stopping trains from Glasgow Central to the Ayrshire port and return, calling at all stations, plus four boat trains connecting with the Arran ferry, and seasonal boat trains connecting with the Isle of Man steamer. There were no trains on Sundays. The branch from Giffen to Kilbirnie saw a regular service of nine trains on weekdays with two extra on Saturdays each way (no trains on Sundays). The branch to Irvine from Kilwinning saw eight trains each way, with two extra on Saturdays. However, there appeared to be a decline

Site of Giffen Junction, Caledonian Railway, Lanarkshire and Ayrshire section (25 October 2007).

Giffen, looking north (25 October 2007).

66

during the 1920s and it wasn't long before economies were made.

The two branches from Lanarkshire and Ayrshire to Irvine Bank Street (in July 1930) and to Kilbirnie (in December 1930) were closed to passengers. Goods services to Kilbirnie South ceased on the same day. In July 1932, local passenger trains were discontinued south of Uplawmoor and the intermediate stations at Lugton High, Giffen, Auchenmade, Kilwinning East, Stevenston Moorpark, Saltcoats North and Ardrossan North, were closed completely. The terminus at Ardrossan Montgomerie Pier was kept open, and boat trains connecting with the steamers at Ardrossan continued, as did goods traffic to the intermediate stations. The line was kept open south of Uplawmoor by a handful of daily boat trains and goods trains.

The Irvine branch closed altogether in June 1939 when the goods service was discontinued.

On the remote Holehouse Junction to Rankinston section, in 1927 an experimental service using a steam railcar was tried and a new halt opened at the hamlet of Cairntable. The railcar did not last long, but Cairntable remained open until the line was closed on 1 April 1950. Immediately prior to closure, Rankinston 'enjoyed' a service of two departures (at 8.17am to Patna via Holehouse Jn with a connection to Ayr, and 4.45pm direct to Ayr via Belston Junction and Annbank Junction). There was an extra train at 1.37pm to Holehouse with the usual connection to Ayr. Arrivals were at 7.53am (from Holehouse Junction, with a connection from Ayr), and 4.44pm from Dalmellington via Holehouse. The extra Saturday train arrived at 1.22pm. With such a sparse service, to and from a small upland village with a population of a few hundred, this was never going to be a big-earning railway, even taking into account the coal traffic it generated.

A further economy was made in 1947, when a connection was made to the ex-G&SWR line at Ardeer near Stevenston, which enabled boat trains for Montgomerie Pier to run from Glasgow down the ex-G&SWR line, rendering the ex-CR line south of Uplawmoor largely superfluous, apart from the little goods traffic left serving Giffen, Gree Goods,

Site of Giffen Station, closed 4 July 1932 (25 October 2007).

Site of Lissens Goods Station (closed 30 March 1953) looking north (12 August 2013).

Modern building on the site of Kilwinning East Station, closed 4 July 1932 (1 May 2013).

Site of Ardrossan North Station, closed 4 July 1932 (18 February 2009).

Auchenmade, Lissens Goods and Kilwinning East. The line from the new connection at Stevenston, 3½ miles north to Kilwinning East, was closed entirely. The line south from Lugton (where there was a connection to the Kilmarnock–Barrhead line) to the new connection at Stevenston was closed by the autumn of 1951.

The LMS made economies on the ex-G&SWR lines also. Passenger traffic was steadily being lost to the improving road network and there was keen competition from the rapidly developing bus system. Whilst there was little impact on the commuter traffic to Glasgow, the local and rural routes within Ayrshire were feeling the effect of increased competition from road transport.

More Closures

The first railway to suffer from low passenger numbers was the Maidens and Dunure Light Railway. Opened as recently as 17 May 1906, along with the Turnberry Hotel, the line was closed to passengers on 1 December 1930. Stations at Alloway, Heads of Ayr, Dunure, Knoweside, Balchristion, Glenside and Maidens were closed, after a life of just over twenty-four years. Again, the line had a very sparse passenger timetable in 1922, the last year of the Glasgow and South-Western Railway, with only six return trips per day over the line, and an extra one on Saturdays. There was also a non-stop (between Ayr and Turnberry) train from Glasgow St Enoch aimed at patrons of the luxury Turnberry Hotel. The trains were slow (70min to cover the 21¾ miles between Ayr and Girvan) and a common complaint from the locals was that the trains did not run at particularly convenient times, but in reality, buses and the private motor car had made serious inroads into the line's custom.

The line was briefly re-opened to passengers on 4 July 1932 but only as a through route for the Turnberry trains – no intermediate stations were reopened. That situation lasted only until 31 May 1933 when the Alloway Junction to Turnberry section reverted to goods only. The section from Girvan to Turnberry, to serve the hotel, retained a dedicated passenger service until, as a wartime economy, it ceased on 2 March 1942, never to be reinstated. However, the line was retained throughout for goods traffic.

The short Catrine branch from the G&SWR main Kilmarnock–Dumfries–Carlisle line at Brackenhill near Mauchline closed to passengers on 3 May 1943,

Caledonian Railway 'Jumbo' passing the site of Monkton Station with a northbound goods train (late 1950s).
BILL HAMILTON

as a wartime economy, but passenger trains never returned to Catrine, apart from 'specials', although goods traffic continued into the 1960s.

The railway from Darvel to Strathaven, opened in 1905, never really realized its potential as a direct route from Lanarkshire to Ayrshire. It had next to no intermediate traffic, and it closed entirely between the two towns on 25 September 1939, when the stations of Loudounhill, Drumclog and Ryeland saw their last trains. The final train timetable saw only three trains per day linking Strathaven and Darvel, with an additional service on Saturdays.

During the period, a few sparsely used wayside stations on busier lines were closed: Monkton (between Prestwick and Troon) closed to passengers on 28 October 1940, with Prestwick station only 1 mile away and nine trains calling each way, all Ayr–Kilmarnock locals. Goods continued to be handled until 3 May 1960. Monkton village, which ended up being right alongside the main runway at Prestwick Airport, was ¾ mile from its station.

Tarbolton (between Annbank Junction and Mauchline) closed to passengers on 4 January 1943, closing to goods on 6 January 1964. Tarbolton village was 1½ miles from its station. Latterly, only four Muirkirk–Ayr trains called at this rural station, with the same number the opposite way. There was an extra working on Saturdays, and as usual no Sunday service.

On the plus side, at the Heads of Ayr, on the northern section of the Maidens and Dunure Light Railway, the Royal Navy had established a training camp during the Second World War. After the War, the Navy disposed of the facility and it was bought by Billy Butlin, the holiday camp developer. Butlin's at Ayr was put on the holiday map for literally hundreds of thousands of people for decades to come. Therefore, for the first holiday season, on 17 May 1947, the first 5 miles of the Maidens and Dunure line reopened to passenger trains between Ayr and a new Heads of Ayr Station, within the boundaries of the newly created Butlin's Holiday Camp. Passenger trains used this line for the next twenty-one years, bringing holidaymakers from all over Scotland and the north of England to Butlin's for their annual summer holidays. Initially Saturdays only, a local service was provided from Ayr, 6 miles away, with certain trains running from Kilmarnock and Glasgow. However, at peak times during the summer, there were through trains onto the branch from Edinburgh, Newcastle upon Tyne and other centres.

BR Standard class 4MT 80051 with a Heads of Ayr to Glasgow Central train, Alloway (early 1960s). BILL HAMILTON

The remote industrial town of Muirkirk suffered during the economic depression of the 1920s, which started a serious decline during the late 1920s and 1930s. The ironworks closed in 1923, leaving only coal-mining at the Kames mine to sustain the remote moorland village. The Second World War brought a reversal in its fortunes, but there was enough usage to keep the sparse passenger service on the lines east to Lanark and westwards to Ayr via Cumnock (A&C) and via Auchinleck and Mauchline open. There was enough work to keep the small locomotive shed open, the effort required during the Second World War seeing an increase in activity, but by the time of nationalization, the lines were struggling, with traffic again declining. Just prior to nationalization, Muirkirk saw four trains per day to and from Lanark, five trains to and from Auchinleck on the Glasgow and South-Western main line, and a further two trains to Ayr via Cumnock and Annbank Junction (with an extra on Saturdays)

The London, Midland and Scottish Railway closed a few smaller engine sheds, starting with Fairlie Pier in 1930 (Ardrossan taking over), with

Glenbuck Station; first station east of Muirkirk, closed c. late 1950s.
TERRY HARRISON COLLECTION

Ayr taking over from Troon Harbour and Dalmellington in 1935. The shed at Girvan closed during the Second World War, in November 1940, again Ayr taking over its duties. At all these locations, basic facilities such as water were retained.

There were a few new stations opened by the London, Midland and Scottish Railway. A platform for workers' trains only was opened in the Nobels Explosives Works at Ardeer, near Stevenston, on 4 July 1926. This was not open to the general public. Barleith Halt, next to the locomotive sheds on the Darvel branch, was opened to the public on 11 July 1928 (it was provided solely for the use of railway staff and families before that). Cairntable Halt, near Rankinston, opened on 24 August 1928. Holehouse Junction, on the Dalmellington branch, opened to the public sometime in 1937, but as an exchange platform only.

The London, Midland and Scottish Railway inherited all the Glasgow and South-Western Railway's properties and assets – 493½ route miles (nearly 1,144 miles of track), a total of 528 locomotives, 1,604 passenger carriages and 19,252 general goods and mineral wagons. Unfortunately for the 'Sou'west', under the new regime most of the locomotives were deemed non-standard. By 1930 almost half that number had been withdrawn and sent for scrap. By 1939 only fourteen locomotives survived, with fewer than half of that number being taken over by the nationalized British Railways.

The brief twenty-five-year period of the London, Midland and Scottish Railway's reign in Ayrshire did result in one or two line closures, but by and large it was a period of stabilization, even stagnation, briefly halted by the Second World War. By the late 1940s, traffic was declining and the railway network was badly in need of investment.

In a situation largely replicating 1919, the UK's railways, again under government control, had been largely worked to capacity during the Second World War, and although the demands placed on them were much reduced by the end of 1945, massive investment was needed to bring the network, and the locomotives and rolling stock that operated on it, up to standard.

The 'Big Four' did not have the financial resources to upgrade a largely worn-out network without substantial government help. The solution was seen to be nationalization (as with the creation of the National Coal Board for the coal-mining industry in 1947). And so it came to pass that on 1 January 1948 the 'Big Four' ceased to exist and 'British Railways' was born.

Muirkirk Station, closed 5 October 1964.
TERRY HARRISON COLLECTION

CHAPTER 5

Nationalization and British Railways: 1948–98

Early Post-Nationalization Closures

As with the grouping of the railways twenty-five years earlier, the new regime inherited a network of railways in Ayrshire that were suffering from a backlog of maintenance and a lack of investment in motive power and rolling stock, all in the face of declining traffic, particularly passengers on the more sparsely populated lines. The new authorities held a review of loss-making services, and they were quick to act.

The lightly used passenger train service from Dalmellington to Rankinston was an early casualty of nationalization. The last train called at Rankinston on 1 April 1950, when LMS 2P no.40590 worked the 4.15pm from Dalmellington to Ayr. From that date the section from Holehouse Junction to Polquhairn Mine closed completely. The section eastwards to Belston Juction remained open for coal traffic.

The lightly used, as far as passenger trains were concerned, A&C line was another early casualty of the BR economies: passenger services from Muirkirk to Ayr via Cumnock and Ochiltree were withdrawn on 10 September 1951. The collieries along the line justified its retention until 7 March 1964, when the section from Cronberry to Dykes Junction was closed completely. Whitehill Pit closed in early 1966, rendering the Belston Junction to Dykes Junction line redundant. The Rankinston line as far as Littlemill Pit survived until January 1975, when the pit closed and the railway east of Drongan closed entirely.

Rankinston Station, on the Holehouse Junction (on the Dalmellington branch) to Belston Junction (on the A&C) line closed on 3 April 1950. The line from Holehouse closed completely on that date, while the line eastwards to Belston Junction remained open for coal traffic, serving the Littlemill and Polquhairn Collieries from Belston Junction on the A&C line. The most famous trains during the 1950s and early 1960s were the coal trains worked by two Caley 0-6-0 goods engines, nicknamed 'the Twins', subsequently by LMS Hughes 'Moguls' (or 'Crabs'), Black 5s, BR standards and, up to closure, various diesels of classes 20, 25, 26 and 27.

The mines were closed by late 1974 and the railway from Drongan to Belston and up to Littlemill closed on 28 July 1975.

Against the trend, in 1959 BR built a 4-mile branch from Drongan up to the new NCB colliery at Killoch, on the main A70 Ayr–Cumnock road. This colliery closed in 1986, but the washing and blending plant was retained to process locally mined opencast coal. Until 2013, the line from Annbank

LMS 'Fairburn' class 4MT 42196 at Annbank station with a railtour (June 1962).
TERRY HARRISON

to Drongan and onwards to Killoch saw heavy coal trains several times a day; there are still a handful per week now.

Traffic to the declining industrial town of Muirkirk came under scrutiny, with two separate routes to Ayr: via Mauchline on the G&SWR main Kilmarnock–Dumfries–Carlisle line, and a little more directly via Cumnock and Drongan; this latter closed to passengers on 10 September 1951. The route to Auchinleck, which left the A&C at Cronberry, was closed to passengers a little earlier, on 3 July 1950. Kames Colliery in Muirkirk kept the railway open from Auchinleck via Cronberry until its closure in December 1968, the railway closing shortly thereafter on 10 February 1969. The section from Auchinleck to Cronberry remained open for freight until 6 December 1976, latterly serving the remote Cairn Mine. Passenger trains eastwards to Lanark survived through the early BR period.

Next for closure was the Maidens and Dunure Light Railway, already bereft of passengers since 1 December 1930. It closed entirely to all traffic between Girvan and the new Heads of Ayr Station (provided to serve the seasonal Butlin's holiday traffic) on 28 February 1959, with the little goods' stations at Dunure, Knoweside, Balchriston Siding, Glenside, Maidens, Turnberry, Dipple and Grangeton closing for good. The goods stations at Heads of Ayr, Greenan siding and Alloway followed suit on 7 December 1959, leaving only the seasonal Heads of Ayr passenger traffic surviving.

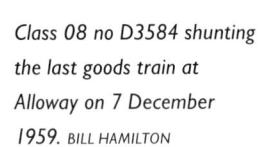

Class 08 no D3584 shunting the last goods train at Alloway on 7 December 1959. BILL HAMILTON

The next closure, at the extreme north of the county, was the short 4-mile branch line from Lugton Junction, on the Barrhead to Kilmarnock Joint line, to Beith Town, on 5 November 1962. Barmill closed to goods on the same day, but goods traffic at Beith Town remained until 5 October 1964.

In the 1950s, some lightly used stations on the main lines closed. On the A&C line, Dumfries House Station closed on 13 June 1949. On the Dalry to Kilmarnock line, Cunninghamhead closed to passengers on 1 January 1950 (goods on 1 February 1960) and Montgreenan on 7 March 1955 (goods on 5 October 1959). On the Glasgow to Ayr line, Beith North closed on 4 June 1960 (goods on 28 October 1963) and Lochside on 4 July 1955 (to both passengers and goods). Lochside did reopen in 1966 and is still open today, renamed Lochwinnoch. Between Ayr and Maybole, both the intermediate stations, Cassilis and Dalrymple, closed on 1 December 1954 (goods at Cassillis on 31 October 1963 and Dalrymple on 6 April 1964). The station at Hurlford, on the main Kilmarnock to Dumfries line, closed on 7 March 1955. Hurlford was served for a few more years by Barlieth Halt (adjacent to the engine sheds, on the Darvel branch).

These were largely piecemeal closures, with British Railways making economies here and there; much worse was to follow with the publication of the Beeching Report in 1963, as we shall see shortly.

Change from Steam to Diesel Traction

The first dozen or so years of British Railways saw many improvements on the busy Ayr to Glasgow and Kilmarnock to Glasgow lines, as well as the G&SWR main line to Dumfries and Carlisle. British Railways had wasted little time in introducing new, modern, steam locomotives, to replace the mostly old, worn-out, motive power inherited from the LMS. The 'standards' ranged from light tank and tender engines for branch-line and local trains, to express locomotives for long-distance work. Various examples of the new classes were put to work, from new, from Ayrshire sheds. Loco-hauled carriages were also designed and produced in a variety of designs,

BR class 126 'Swindon' DMU for the Heads of Ayr passing Greenan Castle Goods (early 1960s). BILL HAMILTON

Ayr Falkland Junction; BR Class 4MT unidentified (early 1960s). ARPG COLLECTION

Ayr Falkland Junction; LMS 'Fairburn' class 4MT 42196 (early 1960s). ARPG COLLECTION

called the 'Mark 1s'. To suit traffic requirements, carriages were built as corridor and non-corridor, and in compartment and saloon configurations, bringing a better level of comfort to the passengers. Sadly, the 'standard' steam locomotives lasted little more than fifteen years, but the new BR Mk 1 coaching stock was seen on passenger trains well into the 1980s.

LNER B1 class 61261 on local passenger train to Ayr at Kilmarnock Station (early 1960s). ARTHUR WILSON

LNER B1 class 61355 approaching Ayr from the south (early 1960s). ARPG COLLECTION

Ayr Falkland Junction; BR Class 4MT 76097 (mid-1960s). ARPG COLLECTION

General view of Ayr shed (mid-1960s). BILL HAMILTON

Diesel locomotives first started appearing in Ayrshire in 1957, with the new BR/Sulzer Type 2 (later class 24) on mineral (coal) traffic to/from Glasgow. Gradually, other early types, such as BR/Sulzer Type 4 'Peak' (class 45) and English Electric Type 4 (class 40), appeared on freight traffic. Apart from 'specials', steam remained firmly in charge of passenger workings.

RIGHT: *Approaching Ayr Station from the north (1961).* BILL HAMILTON

BELOW: *BR 40011 shunts empty stock at Largs to work the return 13.40 to Carlisle (14 August 1976).* ARTHUR WILSON

BR class 40 arrives at Ayr from Waterside (late 1970s). JIM DAVIDSON

BR class 47 D1992 heads the 16.28 Ayr (ex-Stranraer) to Newcastle train at Hawkhill Junction (July 1972). ARTHUR WILSON

BR class 20 8098 at St Marnock (Kilmarnock) (16 May 1973).
JIM DAVIDSON

BR class 126 'Swindon' DMU on an Ayr to Glasgow Central train on the Troon avoiding line near Lochgreen Junction (20 November 1982).
ARTHUR WILSON

BR class 126 'Swindon' DMU passes Troon Old with a Glasgow Central–Stranraer train (20 November 1982).
ARTHUR WILSON

BR class 126 DMU departs Prestwick for Glasgow Central (mid-1970s).
ARPG COLLECTION

That changed in August 1959 when BR Swindon built 'Inter-City' type diesel multiple units (later class 126), which took over the Glasgow St Enoch to Ayr, Girvan and Stranraer workings. The earlier series of Swindons had been introduced in 1956 between Glasgow Queen Street and Edinburgh Waverley via Falkirk High, replacing steam trains, with great success. Along with a new, regular interval timetable, the new diesel multiple units (DMUs) in green livery with yellow lining proved to have

BR class 20 on tracklifting during singling of the Kilmarnock to Troon line, on the outskirts of Kilmarnock (late 1974). JIM DAVIDSON

ABOVE: BR class 27 with a track lifting train, Dalry–Kilmarnock line, near Cunninghamhead (mid-1974). JIM DAVIDSON

BELOW: LNER class A3 60072 passing Ayr shed (late 1950s). BILL HAMILTON

BR diesel electric locos 25023, 228, 20104 and 108 at Ayr shed (25 May 1979). ARPG COLLECTION

BR 27409 and snowploughs at Ayr Shed Open Day (29 October 1983). ARTHUR WILSON

similar success in Ayrshire: passenger numbers increased and the journey time was reduced by up to 15min over the 41½ miles from Ayr to Glasgow St Enoch, due to their superior acceleration from station stops.

Steam traction was on a rapid decline from the late 1950s and early 1960s, with the introduction of diesel multiple units and diesel-electric locomotives. The last regular steam-hauled passenger service was the Kilmarnock to Ardrossan, and when this was withdrawn in April 1964, the decline was almost complete, save for some freight workings. Ardrossan shed closed in 1965, but remained a signing-on point for drivers, mainly of diesel multiple units, until September 1969. Finally, in October 1966, steam locomotives working from both Ayr and Hurlford sheds were withdrawn, which meant the end of steam in Ayrshire and the south-west of Scotland. For Hurlford it really was the end, but Ayr had a future for a further forty-four years, after modification, as a diesel motive power depot, dealing with both multiple units and locomotives.

The Beeching Report – Further Drastic Closures

The economies and closures of the immediate post-nationalization era, coupled with the modernization of the 1950s, proved insufficient to reduce the financial losses by British Railways generally. By 1960, the cumulative losses on British Railways were £42 million. By 1962, the cumulative losses had increased to £104 million. Further action was deemed required by the UK Government to save the taxpayers' money. Dr Richard Beeching was appointed Chairman of the British Railways Board with a remit to streamline Britain's railways, to reduce the losses and to leave the country with a more efficient system, in keeping with the modern economic conditions prevailing at that time. He was an eminent economist, and Chairman of ICI, with no experience of the railway industry. ICI gave Beeching a five-year leave of absence in order to mastermind the return of the country's railways to greater efficiency and profitability. He set about the task immediately, and the economics of every line in the country were scrutinized.

On 27 March 1963 his first report, *The Reshaping of British Railways*, was published. The proposals were drastic: around 7,000 of the United Kingdom's least-used stations were to be closed, and approximately 5,000 route miles of railway were to be closed to passengers, with severe job losses in the industry.

The railways of Ayrshire were not exempt from this, and several branch lines were proposed for closure, together with local trains on the Glasgow and South-Western's main line south of Barrhead. Even the Glasgow and South-Western's magnificent terminus in Glasgow city centre, St Enoch, wasn't spared (it closed to passengers on 27 June 1966 and completely on 5 June 1967).

By the start of 1964, closures were approved for the Dalmellington branch, the Darvel branch and the cross-country line from Kilmarnock to Irvine, and on 6 April of that year the last passenger trains ran on those lines. When one looks at the timetables for the last period of operations on those lines, it wasn't hard to see that there were few passengers. From Darvel to Kilmarnock, there were only three trains each way daily, with a departure from Darvel at 07.31 (through to Glasgow, St Enoch), the next departure not until 17.12, and the last train at 18.35. The busier Irvine to Kilmarnock line was little better with eight trains each way, with a couple non-stop between Kilmarnock and Irvine, for Ardrossan Harbour and the Arran ferry. At Dalmellington, departures for Ayr were at 08.18, 13.35 (through to Kilmarnock) and 18.25. It is little wonder that with such a sparse service, few people took the train.

Later that year, the passenger link from Muirkirk to Lanark was withdrawn, leaving Muirkirk at the end of a freight-only line from Auchinleck on the G&SWR main line.

One of Beeching's policies was to close the remaining intermediate stations on main lines, ridding them of slower, local trains, thus freeing up capacity to improve timings for longer-distance, express trains. Thus, on 6 December 1965, local trains were withdrawn between Kilmarnock, Dumfries and

Mauchline up (southbound) Station building (1971).
STUART RANKIN

Carlisle, and (in Ayrshire) stations at Mauchline, Auchinleck, Cumnock and New Cumnock were closed. At Mauchline, for example, there were southbound departures (to Dumfries and Carlisle) at 07.44, 14.57 and 18.34, northbound departures (to Kilmarnock and Glasgow, St Enoch) being at 05.25 (for Kilmarnock and Ayr), 07.53, 13.11 and 20.15. This was hardly a frequent service that would have attracted much custom.

Similarly, north of Kilmarnock, all the stations to Barrhead were closed on 7 November 1966. For Ayrshire, this meant trains no longer called at Kilmaurs, Stewarton, Dunlop and Lugton. For Stewarton and Dunlop, this was a cut too far, and those two stations were quickly reopened on 5 June 1967, for one train (to pick up only) in the morning to Glasgow and one train (to set down only) in the evening, obviously for the benefit of commuters

Auchinleck Station building (April 1971). STUART RANKIN

New Cumnock Station building (April 1971). STUART RANKIN

only. Kilmaurs also reopened, but much later, on 12 May 1984. These stations did have a dozen trains each way, but any custom that they attracted did not save the stations from closure. Happily, as we will see, in 2015 there is a half-hourly service on the Kilmarnock to Glasgow central line throughout the day and evening.

The seasonal Heads of Ayr branch did not escape the cuts. Since reopening in 1947, the remaining stub of the Maidens and Dunure Light Railway, the 3½ miles from Alloway Junction, south of Ayr to Heads of Ayr (for the Butlin's Holiday Camp) took thousands of holidaymakers to Butlin's, but by the early to mid-1960s they came increasingly by car. Passenger numbers dropped steadily and British Rail withdrew passenger services at the end of the 1968 holiday season. Heads of Ayr saw its last train on 16 September 1969: a three-car Swindon class 126 diesel multiple unit departed for the short journey to Ayr at 15.15. Thereafter, a bus link was provided from Ayr Station for the holidaymakers.

Even the local service linking Ayrshire's two largest towns, only 17 miles apart, Ayr and Kilmarnock, was a surprising candidate, as the trains linked Kilmarnock with the seaside towns of Prestwick, Troon and Barassie along the way, calling at the intermediate stations at Gatehead and Drybridge. This was not a country backwater with a handful of trains; at the time of closure there was a comprehensive service of thirteen trains each way every day except Sundays. This was a prolonged closure due to fierce local protests, including the then Ayr County Council, but finally BR got their way and trains ceased between the two towns on 3 March 1969. The 8 miles between Barassie Junction (a mile north of Troon) on the Glasgow to Ayr railway, and Kilmarnock, Scotland's oldest railway, became freight only from that date.

After that date, the large station at Kilmarnock was served by only seven daily departures to Glasgow Central and five southbound departures to Dumfries, Carlisle and beyond. Thankfully the situation has improved since then.

Renaissance

In 1973, the Kilmarnock area underwent further rationalization to reflect the decline in traffic as a result of the Beeching closures, although this time, the term 'modernization' could be applied. The remaining manual signal boxes were closed and the track layout rationalized. The 'Joint' line to Barrhead was singled, save for a passing loop retained at Lugton, which was more than adequate to cater for the few remaining trains to Glasgow, and the double-track main line to Dalry, on the Ayr–Glasgow line was closed altogether on 2 October 1973. This was surprising as it had not been recommended for closure under Beeching. The by now freight-only line to Barassie Junction was also singled.

Passenger trains returned to the Barassie–Kilmarnock line on 5 May 1975, when the Stranraer–London Euston night-time sleeper train 'the Paddy' was diverted from the Ayr–Mauchline line (it had run directly from Stranraer to Dumfries until the closure of the 'Port Road' via Newton Stewart in June 1965). By the mid-1980s a daytime 'Paddy' had also started using the line, together with summer Saturday-only holiday trains from Stranraer to Scarborough and Morecambe. There was also a daily Ayr to Carlisle and return train, as well as a Glasgow to Ayr via Kilmarnock early evening train (with no corresponding return working). The Sprinter revolution in October 1988 saw the withdrawal of the daytime 'Paddy' Stranraer–London Euston train, to be replaced with a return working to Newcastle. Further local trains were introduced in 1998 with the launch of the 'Burns Line', the introduction of a Kilmarnock–Girvan service, an extension of the Glasgow–Kilmarnock local service and the re-routing of some Glasgow–Stranraer trains, which ran via Paisley. The intermediate stations at Gatehead and Drybridge were not reopened. The Kilmarnock–Troon railway, the oldest in Scotland, had a passenger service once again.

By the late 1970s, the situation in Ayrshire had settled down to its reduced post-Beeching state. With the closures complete, the lines that were left were operated by ageing diesel trains, both locomotive-hauled on the main line to Carlisle and beyond, and diesel multiple units on the lines to the coast and beyond to Stranraer. By the early 1980s, British Rail had decided that a general upgrading and development of the system that was left was necessary.

BR class 45 45034 leaves Kilmarnock for Glasgow Central (March 1976).
ARTHUR WILSON

BR class 45 D49 heads a London Euston to Glasgow Central sleeper train at Kilmarnock (1 October 1974).

BR class 50s 430 and 408 on a diverted London Euston to Glasgow Central service north through Kilmarnock; failed D1708 in bay (October 1971).
ARTHUR WILSON

BR class 108 DMU at Kilmarnock (early 1970s).
JIM DAVIDSON

BR class 47 D1708 heads a diverted car train ex-Elderslie south through Kilmarnock (October 1971).
ARTHUR WILSON

ABOVE: *BR class 120 DMU at Ayr (28 September 1986).*

BR class 107 DMU in Strathclyde Transport livery at Ayr (28 May 1988).

Strathclyde Passenger Transport Executive

In 1972, the Greater Glasgow Passenger Transport Executive (GGPTE) was established to oversee public transport provision in Glasgow and outlying areas. This was to include rail passenger transport. Glasgow has the largest suburban railway system in the United Kingdom outside London; the lines in Ayrshire, to Kilmarnock and Ayr, and the branch to Largs and Ardrossan are included in this area. By this time, all trains in the area were painted BR blue, and from the mid-1970s 'GG' and 'Trans-Clyde' logos appeared on rolling stock, along with the BR double-arrow logo. Towards the end of the 1970s, multiple units started appearing in blue/grey.

In 1983, British Rail launched the 'ScotRail' brand, to cover all internal train services within Scotland. This name appeared on timetables, trains, station signs and publicity. Also in 1983, GGPTE became Strathclyde Passenger Transport Executive (SPTE) and electric and diesel multiple-unit trains started appearing in a striking new orange and black livery. There were also proposals to expand the local Strathclyde rail network, which meant the reopening of stations on existing lines.

BR class 25 comes off the Troon line at Kilmarnock with a Stranraer to Carlisle parcels train (25 September 1978).
MATT MILLER

BR class 47 heads away from Kilmarnock with a train to Stranraer (25 September 1978).
MATT MILLER

LEFT: *BR class 107 DMU at Kilmarnock (7 February 1989).*

BELOW: *BR class 101 Metro-Cammell DMU in refurbished livery; Glasgow Central to Ayr train at Prestwick (4 April 1980).*
ARTHUR WILSON

By the early 1980s, the ageing Swindon-built, class 126 diesel multiple units were becoming dated and showing their age, and were all withdrawn by spring 1983. They were replaced by almost equally old diesel multiple units of classes 107 (BR Derby) and 101 (Metropolitan Cammell), most of which had been refurbished. However, this was not the long-term answer to Ayrshire's busy commuter traffic to Glasgow. In September 1983, the Ayrshire Electrification Project was announced: the line from Paisley (already electrified to Glasgow Central in 1967) to Ayr was to be re-signalled and electrified, together with the branch from Kilwinning to Ardrossan Harbour (later extended to Largs). The line was re-signalled and remaining mechanical signal boxes closed – the entire line being controlled from Paisley signalling centre. Numerous bridges were rebuilt to make enough clearance for the overhead line equipment. In preparation for this, the Troon avoiding line (the original main line from Barassie

Junction to Lochgreen Junction), which was largely superseded by the Troon Loop line, was closed at the end of 1982.

The work on the line to Ayr was completed in the summer of 1986, and the brand-new trains, class 318 electric multiple units built by British Rail Engineering Ltd in York, began their proving runs. The units were delivered in the new SPTE orange-and-black livery. By the end of September, all was ready, and the first day of public services was on Sunday 28 September, when the public were invited to sample the new trains for a flat fare of £1.00 return anywhere. The new electric trains cut 15min off the Ayr–Glasgow journey times, and further increased traffic on an already busy line. The electrification was extended to Ardrossan Harbour in November, and finally to Largs on 19 January 1987. The station at Ardrossan Harbour (formerly Winton Pier) was resited to save a level-crossing, resulting in the shortening of the branch by a couple of hundred metres, and the station at Ardrossan Town was reopened. As a cost-saving measure, only one line of the Largs branch was electrified from Saltcoats, thus the stations at Ardrossan South Beach, West Kilbride and Fairlie were reduced to a single platform. Largs Station was reduced to two platforms. The line remained double-track to accommodate iron ore and, later, coal traffic from Hunterston Port.

BR 318262 at Ayr with the 09.45 Ayr–Glasgow Central train (9 April 1988).

Prestwick Airport; 318269 and 318xxx 14.30 Glasgow Central–Ayr (4 September 1999).

An electric train (318258) at Kilmarnock, Kilmarnock Open Day (11 September 1988).

RIGHT: *Ayr on the first day of electric trains (27 September 1986).*

BELOW: *BR 318261 and 318xxx between Saltcoats and Stevenston with a Largs to Glasgow Central train (9 May 1998).*

BR 318269 with the 15.50 Largs to Glasgow Central train; Largs station before the accident (15 August 1987).

The line is worked as double-track for freight trains as far as Hunterston Junction, and single-track for passenger trains to the terminus at Largs.

Nine years after electric trains commenced at Largs, on 11 July 1995, the first train of the day from Glasgow Central, EMU 318264, failed to stop and crashed through the buffers, across the concourse, through the front of the station and onto the main street. Apart from the driver and guard, there was no one on board, and fortunately no one was injured. The front car of 318264 was badly damaged but was eventually repaired and is still in service today. Largs Station did not fare as well – the structural damage was so severe that the canopies had to be totally removed and the platforms became open to the weather. Tickets were sold from a temporary

The new station building at Largs (28 August 2009).

Brand-new BR 156434 departing Kilmarnock for Ayr, Kilmarnock Open Day (11 September 1988).

BR 156436 departing from Troon with an Ayr to Kilmarnock train, Kilmarnock Open Day (11 September 1988).

building for several years until the nature of the reconstruction was agreed; eventually, in 2005, a small ticket office was opened.

Away from the coast, Kilmarnock, given up as a 'commuter' town by the Beeching Report in the 1960s, gained a regular (hourly) interval service to Glasgow Central, together with an infrequent direct train service (eight per day) to Ayr and Girvan. The electric 'revolution' on the nearby Ayr line passed Kilmarnock by, but in 1988 came the announcement that new trains would come into service in the autumn to replace the near thirty-year-old DMUs. Strathclyde PTE had looked at new diesel trains being manufactured at the time, and decided upon the new class 156 'Sprinter' from Metropolitan Cammell, and added a batch of fifteen onto BR's original order for 100. The new trains were again delivered in the striking SPTE orange-and-black livery. To celebrate this announcement, BR held an Open Day in the goods yard in Kilmarnock on 11 September 1988, and offered a shuttle service from Ayr to Kilmarnock, using two of the new diesel multiple units. In October, they were introduced into public service on all south-west Scotland's non-electrified lines, with a new Stranraer/Girvan and Ayr to Kilmarnock, Carlisle and Newcastle service

Kilmarnock Open Day; LMS class 5MT 'Black 5' 5407 (11 September 1988).

Kilmarnock Open Day BR 141111 (11 September 1988).

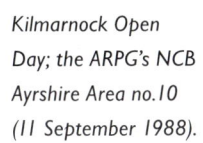

Kilmarnock Open Day; the ARPG's NCB Ayrshire Area no.10 (11 September 1988).

Kilmarnock Open Day; BR 37423 'Sir Murray Morrison' (11 September 1988).

being introduced. The downside of this was the withdrawal of the daytime Stranraer to London Euston, the 'daytime Paddy', depriving towns in the south-west of a direct daytime train to London. The last remaining direct link, the night sleeper from Stranraer to London, was withdrawn on 12 May 1990.

After the Beeching era, with widespread closures of complete lines, and smaller stations on lines that remained open, there was a welcome trend from the early 1980s (intitiated by the SPTE) for stations to be reopened. This was not a new phenomenon, with Lochside Station reopening on 27 June 1966 (as a result of the closure of the Lochwinnoch loop line nearby), and Stewarton and Dunlop Stations on 5 June 1967 (after a brief closure period of seven months), but reopenings started in earnest in the 1980s.

Kilmaurs (closed in November 1966, 2¼ miles north of Kilmarnock) and Auchinleck (closed in December 1965, 14 miles south of Kilmarnock) were reopened on 12 May 1984. A special local

Lochwinnoch; DB Schenker 66111 passing with Prestwick Airport to Grangemouth empty aviation fuel tankers (15 October 2010).

Auchinleck; DB Schenker 66168 passing with coal hoppers (27 February 2014).

service ran for the day, offering passengers a flat fare of 50p to travel to Kilmarnock and Glasgow Central. A class 107 diesel multiple unit in the new orange-and-black SPTE livery worked the service. The very first train to call at Auchinleck, before the official opening, was an excursion, organized by the Ayrshire Railway Preservation Group, from Ayr to Llandudno, hauled by the pioneer class 40, D200 (40122), which is now preserved in the National Railway Museum.

Kilmaurs was served by the hourly Kilmarnock–Glasgow trains, whilst Auchinleck was served by the two-hourly trains south of Kilmarnock to Dumfries and Carlisle. A noteworthy feature of Auchinleck Station is the footbridge, which was 'recycled' from the then closed Crookston on the Paisley Canal line.

Kilmaurs; ScotRail 156508 calls with the 14.42 Glasgow Central–Kilmarnock (7 May 2010).

Freightliner 66553 passes New Cumnock with a southbound coal train (18 October 2005). MAX FOWLER

Next, a few years later, it was New Cumnock's turn to be reconnected to the passenger network. The station platforms were rebuilt and the revitalized station was reopened on 27 May 1991. Beeching had stripped the ex-Glasgow and South-Western main line from Kilmarnock to Dumfries and Carlisle of all its remaining local stations (except Kirkconnel) through the policy of clearing main trunk routes of slow, local trains to increase the speed of expresses, but by the 1980s, the expresses had been withdrawn and the line was left with just a few Glasgow to Carlisle trains. Along with Auchinleck and New Cumnock, two stations further south at Sanquhar and Gretna Green, both in Dumfriesshire, were also reopened.

The last station to open in Ayrshire to date was the long-planned provision of a station adjacent to Prestwick Airport, on 5 September 1994. This was not a reopening, rather a completely new station, on the site of Monkton Junction, for the former direct line to Annbank Junction. From that date, Prestwick Station, just a few hundred metres to the south, was renamed Prestwick Town. This station is unique in Scotland in that it is not owned by ScotRail, although its trains serve it; it is owned by Prestwick Airport.

Railfreight – Decline, Boom, Decline

As far as goods traffic was concerned in Ayrshire, there were huge changes over the British Railways years. The early 1950s saw a number of wayside stations lose their goods handling facility, many of which, with the growth of road transport after the Second World War, saw only occasional use. However, the Beeching Report in 1963 saw just about all remaining local goods yards close by the early 1970s.

The A&C line was kept open, after closure to passengers in 1951, by various coal-mines along its route, but it was progressively closed by mine closures, back to Drongan (where the new line to Killoch Colliery branched off), by 1971. The village of Catrine kept its freight-only service until 6 July 1964, although the occasional 'Enthusiast Special' and 'Sunday School Special' trains ran on the short branch. The line from Cronberry to Muirkirk closed on 7 February 1969 after the closure of Kames Mine. When Cairnhill Mine, near Cronberry, closed in 1976, the railway fell into disuse, although the line up from Auchinleck was not officially closed until 6 August 1978.

By 1980, the only freight traffic left was full trainloads, almost exclusively coal from remaining collieries and opencast mines to power stations. Iron ore for the Ravenscraig Steelworks in Motherwell had been handled at General Terminus, on the south bank of the River Clyde near Glasgow city centre. In 1979, the British Steel Corporation opened a new deep-water port at Hunterston, near Fairlie, between Ardrossan and Largs, which required a short branch. The railway ran right down to the new port (the Low Level) with sidings also serving a loading tower alongside the Largs branch (the High Level). Iron-ore trains, double-headed by Motherwell-based class 37s, commenced in the summer of 1980, and ran via Kilwinning and Paisley to Glasgow and on to Motherwell. Ravenscraig Steelworks was closed, amid great local protests, in 1992, rendering Hunterston Port largely redundant. The Clyde Port Authority took the facility over, and soon began importing large quantities of foreign coal for onward transfer by rail to various power stations in Scotland and in Yorkshire and the Midlands of England. The coal trains initially consisted of two-axle HAA coal-hopper wagons hauled by double-headed class 37s, then progressively class 56 and 60 diesel electric locomotives.

As part of the Ayrshire electrification and re-signalling, the line from Ayr, through Annbank Junction and on to Mauchline, was drastically rationalized. Double-track had remained from Newton Junction to Annbank Junction, where the branch to Killoch Colliery diverged. This was singled, and the line from Annbank to Mauchline (already singled in the 1960s) was closed, including Annbank Junction signal box, on 1 April 1985. The line was disconnected at Annbank and Mauchline. However, the track was left in situ, which was just as well because it was reopened on 17 March 1988, due to the boom in opencast coal originating at the various opencast sites, and imported coal from

Hunterston Low Level; Mainline 60094 'Tryfan' with gypsum wagons (15 August 1998). MAX FOWLER

Transrail 56018 at Hunterston High Level (5 August 1998).
MAX FOWLER

Hunterston Low level; Transrail 56022 with nuclear flasks (July 1998). MAX FOWLER

Hunterston Port. It was this increase in traffic that led to the increased use of, and prevented closure of, the Settle to Carlisle railway in the north of England.

Opened in 1989, the Caledonian paper-mill was built by Finnish company UPM at Meadowhead, between Troon and Irvine. This necessitated the construction of a short branch line and exchange sidings from the Kilmarnock and Troon Railway from a point near Hillhouse Quarry, 1¼ miles east of Barassie Junction. The mill had its own diesel shunter. At first, traffic consisted of timber and china clay slurry inwards, and finished paper outwards. When introduced in 1989, the china clay was delivered from Burngullow, Cornwall, in

Approaching the recently reopened Annbank Junction (7 April 1988).

stainless-steel bogie tanker wagons, nicknamed the 'Silver Bullets', and was the longest freight flow on British Rail. It brought Cornish-based (St. Blazey) class 37s to Ayrshire twice a week. In 2015, the only rail traffic at the mill is the inward flow of china clay slurry, which now comes from Brazil, via Belgium.

Despite the closure of all Ayrshire's deep mines by 1986, substantial amounts of coal were still being produced by means of opencast or surface mining. These were basically 'quarries' but on a massive scale. Advances in mechanized excavating machines and transport vehicles had made this type of mining economical. However, there needed

ABOVE: *Freightliner 66957 passes the old Tarbolton Station (19 March 2014).*

BR class 20s at Mauchline with a coal train from Knockshinnoch to Ayr Harbour (7 April 1988).

BR 37674 departs Caledonian Paper Mill at Meadowhead near Irvine with empty china clay tanks for Burngullow (26 June 1989).
ARTHUR WILSON

to be a location to wash, crush and blend the coal for the end customer; invariably these customers were power stations both in Scotland and south of the border. The existing plant at Killoch, which formerly served the deep mine there, along with its rail link, was retained for this purpose. Another washing facility was required in the New Cumnock area, and one was established in the mid-1980s at the site of Knockshinnoch Mine, to the north-west of New Cumnock. The existing mineral railway from Bank Junction was upgraded and brought back into use. For the next twenty years, vast tonnages of coal were despatched from Knockshinnoch to a large variety of destinations.

Knockshinnoch; 26004 and 26006 arriving (4 June 1990).

In Kilmarnock, by the 1980s, only the coal depot at St Marnock, the Johnnie Walker whisky bottling plant and the oil depot in Riccarton remained. St Marnock depot closed in 1982, but Johnnie Walker continued to despatch some of its famous product by rail until the demise of BR's Speedlink network in 1991, and the spur into the plant became disused. Worse for the town was to follow in 2012 when the plant closed and was quickly demolished. Rail travellers were very familiar with the plant that produced the world-famous whisky brand, as it was located right next to Kilmarnock Station.

As far as freight by rail in Kilmarnock is concerned, only the weekly oil train from Grangemouth to Riccarton remains in 2016.

In the north of the county, the former branch to Beith, and a small remnant of the Caledonian's Lanarkshire and Ayrshire Railway, survived well into the British Railways era. It remained in use for freight trains to serve the munitions depot near Beith, latterly as part of the Speedlink network. After the demise of Speedlink in 1991, the wagon-load nature of the traffic rendered it uneconomical

Unidentified BR class 56 loads at Knockshinnoch (May 1996).
MAX FOWLER

BR 37695, with 26028 and 26036 at the rear, at Annbank Junction with the 'Ayr Restorer' railtour (13 July 1991). CHARLES ROBINSON

BR 26028 and 26036, with 37695 at the rear, at Annbank Junction with the 'Ayr Restorer' railtour (13 July 1991). CHARLES ROBINSON

to British Rail, so the service to Giffen was discontinued and the branch fell into disuse.

The 1990s saw the railways consolidating after the retreats and closures of the 1960s and stagnation in the 1970s. By the mid-1990s, business was good, with most of the passenger trains only ten years old or less. The political will of the Westminster Government of the time dictated that British Rail be broken up and new 'Train Operating Companies' would be set up (ScotRail was one), to be franchised to private companies. The track that the trains run on, as well as the bridges, stations and signalling, would come under a different organization, to be called Railtrack. The era of the nationalized railway was over.

BR class 50s 431 and 449 with a Pathfinder railtour at Kilmarnock (October 2000). MAX FOWLER

EWSR 37415 at Byrehill Junction, Kilwinning with a Branch Line Society railtour (13 August 2000). MAX FOWLER

31465 at Ayr with an A1A Charters railtour at Ayr. (4 August 1997) MAX FOWLER

Waterside: Ayr Restorer railtour, BR 37695 with 26036 and 26028 at the rear (13 July 1991).
CHARLES ROBINSON

CHAPTER 6

Privatization

Passenger Operations

The new privatization era came to Ayrshire at the end of March 1997, when control of all ScotRail train services passed from British Rail to National Express, for a period of seven years. There was little outward sign of the change; even the liveries of the trains remained the same. Strathclyde PTE had changed their livery from the orange-and-black of 1984 to a retro-1950s carmine and cream for both the class 318 EMUs and class 156 'Sprinter' DMUs. However, on the non-Strathclyde class 156s, the National Express house livery of white with a purple window band, aquamarine waistband and terracotta stripe, along with the 'swoosh' logo, appeared. The franchise ran its course until the end of March 2004, when the Aberdeen-based First Group's bid was successful.

During the National Express franchise, forty new trains were introduced in mid-2001 on Ayrshire's

ScotRail 303003 at Ayr, additional service in connection with the Open Golf at Troon (July 1997).
MAX FOWLER

ABOVE: ScotRail 15649 in National Express livery at Kilmarnock with the 07.09 Stranraer to Glasgow Central train (22 April 2006).

ScotRail 156504 and 156500 in Strathclyde PTE carmine-and-cream livery near Kilkerran; the 14.37 Stranraer to Glasgow Central train (18 April 2009).

Prestwick Airport; ScotRail 334006 with an Ayr to Glasgow Central train (6 June 2009).

electric services. They were the three-car class 334 'Juniper' electric multiple units, built by Alstom (successor to Metropolitan Cammell) in Birmingham. There was a protracted commissioning period, culminating in the addition of two extra units by the manufacturer as a gesture of goodwill. The 334s formed Ayrshire's electric services to Glasgow, along with the 1986-built class 318s, together with the Inverclyde services from Glasgow Central to Gourock and Wemyss Bay. The 334s were delivered in a revised carmine-and-cream livery.

First Group took over on 1 April 2004, and apart from the 'swoosh' logo being replaced by First Group's logo on trains and stations, there was little change. The National Express livery on non-Strathclyde EMUs and DMUs was replaced by the 'Barbie' livery. By 2009, Transport Scotland, the Scottish Government Agency dealing with all matters relating to transport in Scotland, had devised a new

Troon; brand-new ScotRail 380105 and 380107 on a test run (31 October 2010).

livery for all trains operating under the ScotRail brand, no matter who the franchise-holder is. The livery is a dark blue, with grey doors and a white dotted 'Saltire' Scottish flag at the carriage ends; light-heartedly called 'SpotRail'.

A further class of new electric multiple units were introduced onto Ayrshire and Inverclyde services in 2010: the class 380 'Desiro' units. Thirty-eight trainsets were ordered, twenty-two three-car units and sixteen four-car units. The individual carriages are 75ft (23m) long, so to accommodate the longer trains to a maximum of seven cars, many stations had to have their platforms extended – many of these stations had their platforms shortened at the 1986 electrification. The units were built by Siemens in Krelfeld in Germany, and brought to the UK through the Channel Tunnel. Enough units were ordered to cover the proposed rail link to Glasgow Airport, a scheme that never came to fruition.

The class 380s had a trouble-free commissioning period, and started in public service in December 2010; they now handle all electrified passenger services on the Ayr–Glasgow line. The class 334s, which had dominated these services for the previous ten years, were progressively refurbished and put to work on the Helensburgh–Glasgow–Bathgate–Edinburgh line. Part of this line was reopened between Airdrie and Bathgate in December 2010.

Although not in Ayrshire, after 150 years of operating cross-channel ferries to Ireland, the ferries operated by Stena and P&O moved to new terminals at Cairnryan in October 2011, leaving Stranraer Harbour Station with no ferry connection and putting the future of the railway south of Girvan in doubt. The timetable south of Ayr to Girvan and onwards to Stranraer was unaffected, but these trains no longer connected with the ferries at Stranraer. Cairnryan is only 6 miles north of (and within sight of) Stranraer, but Transport Scotland provide a bus for foot-passengers from the ferries to take them north to Ayr, where they can get an onward rail connection. The journey by bus takes 1h 15min – about the same time as the train.

Eight years passed since the award of the second franchise in 2007, and on 1 April 2015, after winning the bidding process, Abellio, a division of Dutch National Railways (Nederlandse Spoorweg) became ScotRail's third operator. In Ayrshire and south-west Scotland, improvements include an hourly service from Kilmarnock to Girvan, with every other train going on to Stranraer, giving the Wigtownshire town a train every two hours instead of six per day.

A new requirement of the franchise will be the introduction of 'Great Scottish Scenic Railway' trains on the more famous Highland lines, as well as the Kilmarnock–Dumfries and Girvan–Stranraer lines, operated by steam locomotives.

Freight Operations

On the freight-train operations in Ayrshire, English, Welsh and Scottish Railway (EWSR) bought Transrail in February 1996. TransRail operated mainly on coal traffic. In November 2007, English, Welsh and Scottish Railway was bought by Deutsche Bahn (German Railways) and in January 2009 was rebranded as DB Schenker.

Other private railway operators handling freight (mainly coal) traffic in Ayrshire were Freightliner Heavy Haul, GB Railfreight (GBRf) and Colas Rail Freight, all of whom have a share in the traffic.

When EWSR took over the BR subsidiary companies Transrail, Loadhaul, Mainline and Rail Express Systems, it inherited a fleet of around 1,600 diesel electric locomotines of classes 20, 37, 47, 56, 58 and 59, with an average age of just short of thirty years. Most of these locomotives needed a major overhaul every seven years, and in service the reliability was not satisfactory. To be more competitive, EWSR needed to reduce the operating costs of the older locomotives and increase reliability. As EWSR was an American-owned company, they turned to American technology. British Rail had operated thirteen privately owned (by Foster Yeoman, Amey Roadstone and National Power) class 59 diesel electric locomotives from Electro Motive Diesel (General Motors), since the mid-1980s – the first American motive power to be used in the UK. Their performance had proved to be impressive compared with

Mainline 37248 'Midland Railway Centre' and Loadhaul 37xxx at Newton on Ayr, bound for Killoch (13 July 1997). MAX FOWLER

National Power 59206 on a trial run to to Killoch (6 May 1998).
MAX FOWLER

older, UK designs, so EWSR approached General Motors, who offered an upgraded variation of the class 59 – the class 66. EWSR were satisfied that this would suit their needs and ordered 250 locomotives, to be built at the Electro-Motive Diesel (EMD) plant at London, Ontario, in Canada. The first-class 66 locomotives arrived in the UK in June 1998, and deliveries were complete by December 2001. It took only a few months before the first examples appeared in Ayrshire, initially on the long-distance flows from Hunterston to various power stations in Yorkshire and the Midlands of England, but it was not long before they appeared on the local coal-workings to Knockshinnoch, Chalmerston and Killoch. Within three years, the first- and second-generation diesels had disappeared from Ayrshire.

Initially, all the coal traffic was in the hands of EWSR, but Freightliner (also using class 66 locomotives of their own) made inroads into the expanding coal traffic, with GB Railfreight occasionally winning some short-term contracts. Ayr depot continued to be a signing-on, refuelling and maintenance depot, as well as handling wagon repairs in the old DMU shed.

A new coal-handling terminal was set up at Crowbandsgate, next to New Cumnock station, in 2005. This took processed, opencast coal from several

Stevenston; EWSR 66081 with coal hoppers for Hunterston; first weeks of class 66 operation to Ayrshire (24 April 1999).

BELOW: *Ayr depot; Transrail 60080 'Kinder Scout' and Loadhaul class 60 (July 1997).* MAX FOWLER

Network Rail New Measurement Train re-fuelling at Ayr Depot (6 May 2008).

Site of Ayr Blackhouse Junction; 66527 with coal train from Hunterston (6 March 2008).

EWSR class 08 bringing coal hoppers from Falkland Yard to Ayr Depot for overhaul (April 2004). MAX FOWLER

mines in the New Cumnock and Kirkconnel area, as well as Skares. Coal was taken from the nearby Garleffan site to the loading terminal at Crowbandsgate by conveyor and loaded onto trains. The siding was reached off the up goods loop. There was no connection off the down line, so trains from the south had to pass New Cumnock without stopping, proceed to Mauchline and take the line to Annbank Junction and Ayr. At Ayr, they joined the Glasgow line at Newton Junction, and followed this line up to Barassie Junction, where they turned eastwards over the Kilmarnock and Troon line, to Kilmarnock. There, they joined the main line south for 22 miles, where they reached their destination at New Cumnock, around two hours after they had passed the terminal heading north.

EWSR class 66s, Crowbandsgate, New Cumnock (18 September 2000). MAX FOWLER

PRIVATIZATION

EWSR 66166 at Crowbandsgate coal terminal (19 June 2002).
MAX FOWLER

Kilmarnock Long Lyes; GBRf 66713 runs round bogie coal hopper wagons (5 May 2010).

Kilmarnock Long Lyes; another view of GBRf 66713 running round bogie coal hopper wagons.

113

To avoid this 'tour of Ayrshire', Network Rail cleared the first mile of the old Dalry line north of Kilmarnock Station. This line had been closed in 1973 and dismantled not long after, although a mile and a half was retained for the use of the Engineering Department for testing and training purposes for their track maintenance machines, which were maintained and overhauled at the old Kilmarnock works, adjacent. These sidings became known as the 'long lyes', but by the mid-2000s had been long disused, abandoned and had become very overgrown. In 2009, all this was cleared away, and a loop long enough to handle the largest coal trains was laid. By the spring of 2010, the new 'long lyes' was in use, proving to be a useful addition to the network.

The coal-processing facility at Knockshinnoch was closed around 2005 and dismantled not long afterwards; the line from Bank Junction became disused. However, a new line was built, on the trackbed of an old mineral railway, from a point halfway along the branch, to a new opencast site at Greenburn, keeping the local railway network busy with coal traffic.

In the 2000s, the Ayr to Mauchline line and the branch to Killoch, and the Doon Valley (ex-Dalmellington branch) line to Chalmerston branches remained in use for coal traffic. However, there was a threat from abroad, and cheaper,

New Cumnock; EWSR class 66087 with a coal train at Greenburn opencast (9 July 2004). MAX FOWLER

New Cumnock; EWSR 66087 on the Greenburn branch (9 July 2004). MAX FOWLER imported coal from South and North America, Australia and other parts of the world began arriving in large quantities, leading to an increase in long-distance haulage of imported coal from the Hunterston deep-water port on the Largs branch to power stations in Yorkshire and Derbyshire. This took its toll on local opencast mines and by 2010 production had ceased at Chalmerston, and the branch from Dalrymple Junction, although not formally closed, became devoid of any traffic. Worse was to follow, in May 2013, when Scottish Coal, who operated several opencast mines in Ayrshire, also the Killoch coal-processing plant, went into liquidation. At that point, the only places where locally mined coal was handled by rail were Crowbandsgate and Greenburn, a huge reduction on rail traffic from a few years before.

EWSR (now DB Schenker) had lost much of its traffic to Freightliner Heavy Haul and, as a result, started downgrading its facilities in Ayr. The first sign of things to come was that the class 08 pilot (yard shunter) at Falkland Yard was withdrawn in mid-2008 and shunting was then carried out by main-line locomotives. The crew signing-in point was moved from Ayr Depot to Falkland Yard, and in July 2010, after 131 years in continuous use, Ayr Depot was finally closed – redundant and not needed any more.

In 2012, a new freight-operating company appeared in Ayrshire – on the long-standing flow of the twice-weekly trainload of aviation fuel from the massive Ineos refinery at Grangemouth to the discharge facility on the site of the old Monkton station, next to Prestwick International Airport. Colas Railfreight took over the working from DB Schenker on 1 May. Initially, Colas class 66s were used, but after a few months, much to the delight of local rail enthusiasts, refurbished class 56s were used, bringing the type to Ayrshire's rails for the first time in eleven years.

Colas 56078 passes Troon with a Grangemouth to Prestwick Airport aviation fuel tanker train (18 March 2014).

Infrastructure

Track renewal and maintenance, stations and signalling have remained much the same after prvatization as before. British Rail did much in the 1970s and 1980s to modernize signalling on Ayrshire's two main lines. The Kilmarnock area was rationalized/modernized in 1973/74, with a new power signal box replacing, on the Troon line, Grange, St Marnock's and Shewalton Moss mechanical signal boxes; the box at Gatehead remained open to control the level-crossing. On the main line the boxes at Kilmarnock North, Kilmarnock South and Kay Park Junction were replaced. The line to Dalry was closed and the Troon line singled.

Right into the early 1980s, the very busy Ayr to Glasgow line was still controlled by mechanical signal boxes and semaphore signalling, all very labour-intensive, and maintained out of the S&T works at Irvine. All this was swept away with the electrification and re-signalling scheme, announced by British Rail in 1981. Work started in 1982, and an early casualty was the closure, in November 1982, of the Troon direct line (the original main line to Ayr, superseded in 1892 by the loop line), which had been used by passenger trains not stopping at Troon and by freight trains. The raising of dozens of bridges, track renewal and erection of electrification masts and wiring took place over the miles between Paisley and Ayr, and from Kilwinning and Largs over 3½ years, whilst the normal intensive service operated. Stations were also modernized and, in the case of Dalry, completely rebuilt. All the remaining mechanical boxes on the Ayr–Glasgow line were closed by the inauguration of electrification in September 1986.

However, many mechanical signal boxes survived to be taken over by Railtrack, and its successor, Network Rail. In Ayrshire, south of Ayr you can see signal boxes at Kilkerran (opened in April 1895), south of Maybole, controlling a level-crossing and passing loop, Girvan (opened in 1893) Station and passing loop, and Barrhill Station and passing loop. Barrhill signal box is noteworthy because not only is it the smallest box in Scotland (if not the UK), it is 'second-hand', having been relocated from Portpatrick when the original Barrhill signal box burned down in 1935.

The signal box at Lugton survived the Kilmarnock rationalization of 1974, retained with its semaphores to control the passing loop on the singled line, as well as the junction of the freight-only line to Giffen.

On the main line south from Kilmarnock, signal boxes survive at Hurlford, Mauchline (where the freight-only branch from Ayr joins) and New Cumnock, controlling the station, the branch to Knockshinnoch and Greenburn, and the sidings at Crowbandsgate.

Network Rail undertook a large project in 2007–09 to re-double the line between Lochridge, half a mile south of Stewarton, to the passing loop at Lugton – a distance of 5 miles. The line between Kilmarnock and Barrhead was singled in October 1973. The project cost £34 million and included the re-building of Dunlop and Stewarton Stations back to twin platforms. The works were completed in time for the introduction of the half-hourly Kilmarnock to Glasgow passenger service in November 2009. As part of the re-doubling, the

Kilkerran signal box, opened by the G&SWR in April 1895 (15 November 2007).

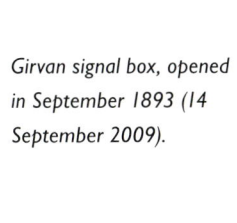

Girvan signal box, opened in September 1893 (14 September 2009).

branch to Giffen, disused since the early 1990s, was disconnected.

It was during this period of upgrading the Lugton to Stewarton section that, on 27 January 2009, a serious accident occurred at a bridge carrying the railway over the Stewarton to Kilmarnock road. The weekly tanker train from Grangemouth to Riccarton, hauled by DB Schenker locomotive 66067, was crossing the bridge, when, during its passage, the bridge collapsed from under it. The rear section of the train was derailed, the bridge collapsing onto the road below. The train consisted of ten bogie tanker wagons, carrying kerosene, diesel and gasoil. Several of the derailed wagons ruptured, and one caught fire. Luckily no one was hurt and, thankfully, there was no road traffic at the bridge at the time. The line was only closed for four weeks. The bridge was due to be replaced, and the new replacement bridge had already been fabricated, so quickly replaced the demolished bridge, which had been in

Mauchline signal box, opened February 1874 (7 April 1988).

Barrhill signal box (ex-Portpatrick) installed 1936 (23 April 2010).

Dunlop reconstructed station; ScotRail 156504 with the 11.57 Kilmarnock–Glasgow Central (9 September 2010).

place since the line opened in 1873. The cause of the collapse was that the ends of the steel beams, which were embedded into the abutments, had corroded away so as to weaken the beams to destruction. This had not been detected during recent rigorous inspections.

Stewarton reconstructed station; ScotRail 156435 with the 14.27 Kilmarnock–Glasgow Central (15 February 2010).

CHAPTER 7

Present Day

So, in previous chapters, we have seen how the railways in Ayrshire evolved, contracted and, in the past thirty-five years, have had something of a renaissance. What of the railways of Ayrshire today, in mid-2015?

Passenger Traffic

Generally, the privatized railways in the county can be said to be thriving, as far as passenger traffic is concerned. Abellio took over the ScotRail franchise on 1 April 2015 and, apart from replacing the 'First' logos on trains and stations with 'Abellio' ones in the first few weeks of the franchise, there has been no noticeable difference.

The two main lines through Ayrshire act mainly as commuter services into Glasgow. The electrified Ayr line has a significant number of passengers visiting the coastal towns of Largs, Saltcoats, Irvine, Troon, Prestwick and Ayr for pleasure, especially at weekends during the summer. Ayr is served by four trains per hour from Glasgow (two stopping and two express), Ardrossan has two trains per hour and Largs has one train per hour. The electrified lines from Glasgow to Ayr, Ardrossan and Largs are operated by Siemens class 380 electric multiple units, introduced in December 2010.

The line from Kilmarnock across to Troon and Ayr is integrated with the service to Girvan and Stranraer. There are currently ten daily trains from Kilmarnock to Ayr (with only eight going the other way), serving Troon, Prestwick Airport, Prestwick Town and Ayr, and most continuing to Girvan and some to Stranraer. The Kilmarnock to Girvan service increased to hourly in December 2015. Although these trains pass Barassie Station, they cannot call there as the platforms on the Kilmarnock line were removed in the late 1970s; they have not been reinstated as they are considered to be on too sharp a curve for modern trains.

The Kilmarnock line, from having a very sparse service to Glasgow up to the early 1980s, now has two trains per hour all day and evening to Glasgow. The station at Kilmaurs was reopened in May 1984. South of Kilmarnock, through Glasgow to Carlisle on the Glasgow and South Western main line, trains serve Auchinleck, New Cumnock, Kirkconnel, Sanquhar, Dumfries, Annan and Gretna Green. Some of these trains continue to Newcastle. South of Ayr, there is a frequent service of eighteen trains to Maybole and Girvan, some originating from Glasgow but most from Kilmarnock, with eight trains continuing to Stranraer. All non-electrified services in the south-west of Scotland have been operated by class 156 'Sprinter' DMUs since October 1988.

ScotRail 380014 approaches Saltcoats with a Glasgow Central to Ardrossan Harbour train (5 July 2013).

ScotRail 380017 passes Glasgow Gailes golf course with a Glasgow Central to Ayr train with Irvine in the background (14 June 2014).

ScotRail 156462 at Bowhouse south of Kilmarnock with a Carlisle to Glasgow Central train (6 March 2014).

In the longer term, probably by 2020, the Glasgow to Barrhead and Kilmarnock (together with the associated branch to East Kilbride) will probably be electrified. All these routes have an intensive service of at least two passenger trains per hour, so electrification would be a logical step. In connection with this scheme, it would be sensible to electrify Scotland's oldest railway, the 8-mile long Kilmarnock and Troon line, linking Kilmarnock with the already electrified Ayr to Glasgow line at Barassie.

In the south of the county, the former railway hotel and golf courses at Turnberry continue to thrive as a top-class, world-renowned holiday destination. The railway serving the resort has long gone, but the five-star hotel continues to attract the wealthy golf tourist. The resort was recently acquired by the Trump organization, which is further upgrading the hotel and golf courses. The main course at Turnberry is a regular venue for the world's greatest golf tournament, the Open, itself a great testament to the vision of the Glasgow and South-Western Railway in the early years of the last century.

Freight Traffic

Since the 1980s, freight traffic, principally the transport of locally mined and imported coal, has provided the bulk of rail-freight traffic in Ayrshire; however, at present much of this traffic has disappeared. The liquidation of Scottish Coal in May 2013 led to the start of the downturn, with the sudden stop in production of coal at several opencast sites, as well as the processing facility at the former mine at Killoch, at the end of the branch from Annbank Junction on the Ayr to Mauchline line. Hargreaves, a private mining company, took over Scottish Coal's assets and started a limited amount of production, so the Killoch branch now sees some use. The other freight-only branch, the former Dalmellington line up the Doon Valley to Chalmerston, has seen no use since the autumn of 2010, when production stopped – at the time it was said for 're-equipping'. Chalmerston remains closed, and the Doon Valley line is unlikely to see further use. Hargreaves also own the opencast mines in the New Cumnock/Kirkconnel area, and coal production is still despatched from the Crowbandsgate terminal near New Cumnock Station.

Imported coal continues to arrive at the Hunterston deep-water port between West Kilbride and Fairlie, generating long-distance flows from Ayrshire to power stations in England. In mid-summer

Freightliner 66606 at Ayr Harbour with cement tankers from Oxwellmains (December 2006). MAX FOWLER

2015, there were paths for daily departures from Hunterston High Level Yard to power stations at West Burton, Ratcliffe, Ferrybridge, Drax, Rugeley B and Fiddlers Ferry. Trains are mostly operated by Freightliner Heavy Haul (FHH), DB Schenker (DBS) and Great Britain Railfright (GBRf). There were also six trainloads of imported coal (operated by DBS) from Hunterston High Level to Longannet Power Station on the banks of the River Forth. However, this will cease in 2016 with the closure of Longannet, announced in March 2015. Another traffic flow, this time from the Low Level Yard, is spent nuclear fuel from Hunterston B Power Station. This is conveyed in nuclear flasks to Sellafield in Cumbria by trains operated by Direct Rail Systems on an occasional 'as required' basis – often weekly. The trains go via Glasgow and down the West Coast main line, via Beattock, as opposed to the Glasgow and South-Western main line via Dumfries.

The remaining stub of the Riccarton loop line remains in use, receiving a weekly oil tanker train from Grangemouth to serve an oil depot in the south

DRS 37218 and 37607 approach Stevenston with Hunterson to Sellafield nuclear flasks (17 September 2014).

DB Schenker 66097 leaves Riccarton with empty fuel tankers for Grangemouth (7 November 2011).

Freightliner 66509 passes Saltcoats with a trainload of imported coal from Hunterston to Cottam power station (20 September 2013).

side of Kilmarnock. The train runs to Kilmarnock via the Barrhead line, as do the return empty tankers. This train normally runs on Monday mornings and was operated by DB Schenker, invariably handled by a class 66 diesel electric locomotive now operated by Colas.

The Caledonian Paper Mill, between Irvine and Troon, receives two trainloads of china clay per week via the short branch line from the Kilmarnock and Troon line. The china clay has quite a journey to reach Ayrshire. It is imported from Brazil, by sea to Belgium. From there, it is loaded onto bogie tankers and runs to Irvine via the Channel Tunnel, Dollands Moor Yard, London, the West Coast main line to Mossend Yard near Glasgow, thence down the Ayr line to Falkland Yard, Ayr, where it reverses again and heads back north for 10 miles on the final leg to Irvine. The other raw material for the factory is timber; however, none of this comes in by rail, nor does the finished product, glossy paper, leave by rail – this is all dealt with by road traffic at present.

Another longstanding freight flow is the Grangemouth to Prestwick Airport aviation fuel train. The fuel terminal was originally located at Glenburn, on the remaining stub of the line from Monkton to Mossblown Junction, on the Ayr to Mauchline line. This was closed in 1971 and a new terminal, a little nearer the airport, was opened at the site of Monkton Station. The train operates twice a week, Tuesdays and Fridays, according to demand from the airport. After privatization, the train was operated by EWSR/DBS, then, in May 2013, Colas Railfreight took over, currently using class 56 locomotives, thereby bringing some welcome 'heritage traction' to Ayrshire.

Troon–Lochgreen; Colas 56094 passes with Grangemouth to Prestwick Airport aviation fuel tankers (12 September 2014).

The remnants of the Beith branch from Lugton, connecting onto the short stretch of the Caledonian's Lanarkshire and Ayrshire line to Giffen to serve RNAD Beith (Royal Naval Armaments Depot – now known as Defence Munitions), lies intact but abandoned and heavily overgrown. In fact, during the re-doubling of the Lugton to Stewarton section in 2008–09, the branch was disconnected. The last regular traffic on the branch was in 1991.

Another rail freight terminal in Ayrshire is at a large pharmaceutical factory at Dalry, which, up till earlier in 2015, generated inward and outward rail traffic, but sadly this has now ceased.

Specials/Excursion Traffic

The scenic delights, as well as several attractive seaside towns, of Ayrshire and the Clyde coast have always attracted much leisure traffic to Ayrshire's railways, as well as outward traffic to other parts of Scotland and England (and even Wales) for Ayrshire residents to enjoy a day out by rail. The highly scenic line to Stranraer from Ayr, and especially south of Girvan, attracts at least one excursion train every year. The annual 'Great Britain' steam-hauled rail tours have visited Stranraer three times in recent years, bringing the sight of double-headed Stanier 'Black 5s' to the gradients south of Ayr. Many tours, steam or vintage diesel-hauled, use Ayrshire as part of a circular tour; for example, from Carlisle up the Beattock route to Glasgow, and back again via the Glasgow to Ayr line, from Newton on Ayr up the freight-only line to Mauchline, and down the Glasgow and South-Western main line through Dumfries back to Carlisle, and thence south.

Once or twice a year, special excursions originate in Ayrshire, either from Kilmarnock or Ayr. Most popular is a run up to Glasgow, and onwards along the north bank of the Clyde to Helensburgh and onwards up the West Highland railway to Fort William, and westwards to Mallaig; or, up to Perth,

LNER A4 class 60009 'Union of South Africa' passes Troon with the 06.16 Crewe–Crewe railtour (27 September 2014).

LNER K4 class 61994 passes Troon with the 07.48 Barnhill–Carlisle railtour (22 September 2014).

DRS. 66424 with the diverted Grangemouth to Daventry Tesco container train past Troon (11 April 2009).

northwards to Inverness, then westwards to Kyle of Lochalsh, these passing through some of Scotland's finest scenery. It is a long day out; you can expect to be away for up to 18 hours.

Excursions are also run south of the border, recent destinations being York (via the scenic Glasgow and South-Western and Settle and Carlisle lines), Chester and Llandudno. These trains are formed with ex-British Rail Mark 1- or 2-hauled carriages, traction provided by First generation diesels (class 37 or 47) and are popular with members of the general public, as well as railway enthusiasts. They are organized by private railtour companies, such as Compass, Pathfinder or the Scottish Railway Preservation Society. Incidentally, 'First generation diesels' refers to the initial wave of diesel locomotives and multiple units introduced in the late 1950s and early 1960s to replace steam traction.

Troon; DB Schenker 66156 passes Troon with the diverted 08.47 Dalston–Grangemouth empty fuel tankers (9 May 2015).

Diversions

The Glasgow and South-Western main line from Carlisle to Glasgow via Dumfries and Kilmarnock, and even via the Mauchline to Ayr freight-only line, is regularly used for diverted traffic if the main West Coast main line via Beattock is blocked for maintenance. Where possible, some passenger trains are diverted through Kilmarnock, but this is difficult as the partially single, partially double Barrhead to Kilmarnock section is already used to capacity. Any diverted freight traffic usually comes up the Nith Valley from Dumfries, at Mauchline heads for Ayr, then up the Ayr to Glasgow and onwards. Examples of this in mid-2015 were the Dalston to Grangemouth empty tanker train, and the Daventry to Mossend container train.

Network Rail

Railways generally need to be maintained to the highest standard, and Ayrshire is no exception, especially the busy lines from Glasgow to Ayr and Kilmarnock. Network Rail regularly run special trains, packed with computers and electronic equipment, to monitor all aspects of the infrastructure: the state of the track, ballast, radio communications and overhead line equipment on electrified lines. The 'New Measurement Train', a converted Inter-City 125 high-speed train, makes regular runs on the Glasgow to Ayr line, and the Glasgow and South-Western main line. Other specialist trains are locomotive-hauled, usually by class 37 or occasionally a class 31, also a customized 'Sprinter' diesel multiple unit; all are regular visitors to Ayrshire's railways.

It is a measure of how much the railways of Ayrshire have been upgraded and modernized that there are only seven traditional signal boxes with semaphore signals left in Ayrshire: at Lugton on the Kilmarnock to Barrhead line, Hurlford, Mauchline and New Cumnock on the Glasagow and South-Western main line south of Kilmarnock, and at Kilkerran, Girvan and Barrhill on the Stranraer line south of Ayr. All main lines are laid with continuously welded rail, with concrete or steel sleepers, with some jointed track still remaining on the Stranraer line south of Ayr.

Relatively few stations have reopened in Ayrshire since the closures of the Beeching era; only Stewarton and Dunlop on the Kilmarnock to Barrhead line (they were only closed for a matter of months

Troon Lochgreen; Network Rail measurement train passes Lochgreen with the 13.13 Ayr to Ayr Falkland Yard via Carlisle (21 April 2015).

BELOW: *31106 passing Polnessan en route to Dunaskin on the Chalmerston branch (3 March 2011).*
ARTHUR WILSON

Network Rail track testing DMU 950001 on the Greenburn branch (21 January 2005). MAX FOWLER

between 1966 and 1967, during the Beeching era), Lochside (replacing Lochwinnoch, and renamed Lochwinnoch in 1985) in 1966, Auchinleck (1984) and New Cumnock (1991), south of Kilmarnock on the Dumfries line, and an entirely new station at Prestwick Airport (1994). A resited Ardrossan Harbour Station was opened in January 1987, along with a single-platform Ardrossan Town on the same date, upon electrification of the branch. Various further reopenings have been talked about, notably Mauchline, south of Kilmarnock, and the Ayr Hospital, south of Ayr, but no further openings of new stations have happened in Ayrshire.

Abandoned Railways

As in all parts of the United Kingdom, Ayrshire has its fair share of abandoned railways. Most lines that have been closed and dismantled have been left and are returning to nature, or have been taken over by farming. However, several sections have been made into pathways/cycleways, making it easier for explorers to travel on routes where trains once ran.

The line that ran between Irvine and Kilmarnock is now a cycleway; at the site of Crosshouse Station it joins the Dalry to Kilmarnock route for the last couple of miles into Kilmarnock. Apart from bridges and viaducts, very little remains to tell the walker/cyclist that the route was ever a railway, all traces of Dreghorn, Springside and Crosshouse stations having vanished.

South of Ayr, in Alloway, a couple of miles of the Maidens and Dunure Light Railway has been made into a cycleway, including through the site of Alloway Station, through the tunnel and over the ornamental viaduct over the River Doon.

In Saltcoats and Ardrossan, the last few miles of the old Caledonian Railway's route can be cycled and walked. Further north, from Kilbirnie all the way to Elderslie, the Lochwinnoch loop line is now a cycleway. Here, the platforms of the old station at Kilbirnie survive (along with that at Kilbarchan in Renfrewshire) but the station site in Lochwinnoch itself has disappeared under a housing estate.

For the more intrepid explorer, other abandoned lines are perfectly walkable, some with a degree of difficulty and with the landowners' permissions, and for some this is a challenging, healthy and rewarding pastime.

Crosshouse Station, closed 18 April 1966, looking west, with BR Wickham diesel railbus on an Ardrossan–Kilmarnock service (early 1960s). STUART RANKIN

CHAPTER 8

Industrial Railways and Preservation

Industrial Railways

In previous chapters, we have seen that many of Ayrshire's railways were built with the particular aim of enabling coal to be transported from the mines, mostly in remote areas, to the towns and cities. Passenger services were also run on these lines, almost as an afterthought. The railway could not directly serve every coal-mine, so the mining companies built, operated and maintained their own railways to connect to the 'main line'.

The most extensive industrial railway, and certainly the most long-lived, was the Waterside system in the upper Doon Valley, developed in the 1840s by the Dalmellington Iron Company to link its various coal- and iron-ore mines in the locality with the ironworks at Dunaskin, between Patna and Dalmellington. Initially the line ran from Sillyhole, near Dalmellington, to the iron furnaces at Dunaskin, eventually extending from Pennyvenie Mine above Dalmellington, down to Dunaskin and onwards to Houldsworth Mine, 1½ miles south of

NCB no.17 (Barclay 1338 of 1917) near Cutler sidings, Waterside (28 December 1976). JIM DAVIDSON

NCB no.19 (Barclay 1614 of 1918) at Waterside (1976).
ANDREW ARNOT

Patna. When the Glasgow and South-Western Railway opened its branch from Ayr in May 1856, the Waterside system was already well established – the first steam locomotive having arrived in 1854, drawn by a team of horses all the way from Ayr, 12 miles along the road. Throughout the history of the industrial railways in the Doon Valley, the vast majority of locomotives were purchased from the Kilmarnock firm of Andrew Barclay, Sons & Co. in Kilmarnock.

The ironfounding at Dunaskin ceased in 1921, and the ironworks was replaced by a brickworks. The Waterside system continued in operation for as long as coal was mined in the Doon Valley. At Dunaskin were located the washery, where the coal was processed, engine shed, workshops and wagon-

NCB no.24 (Barclay 2235 of 1953) and BR class 20 at Dunaskin Exchange sidings (c. 1977). JIM DAVIDSON

NCB no.17 (Barclay 1338 of 1917) at Waterside Washery (1976).
ANDREW ARNOT

repair shop. It was also the location of exchange sidings, where the main line took over the trainloads of coal to take them down the branch to Ayr and beyond. The system became nationalized in 1947, when all mines came under the control of the National Coal Board.

There was a part of the Waterside system that was detached from the rest, to serve the company's Meadowhead Mine at Coylton, a few miles east of Ayr beside the main road to Cumnock. The line ran from Potterston Junction, just south of Dalrymple Viaduct, and headed north-eastward by way of Purclewan Mill and past Martnaham Loch till it reached the mine, on the outskirts of Coylton. To take the production of the mine to Dunaskin, the Dalmellington Iron Company's trains had running powers over the G&SWR's Dalmellington branch between Potterston Junction and Waterside. The Dalmellington Iron Company's Barclays-built industrial locomotive that worked the railway

Dunaskin; NCB no.17 (Barclay 1338 of 1917) (8 April 1977). JIM DAVIDSON

to Coylton became known as the 'Coylton Nanny' and railway on which it worked became known as 'the Nanny Line'. It became redundant in the early 1930s when Meadowhead Mine closed, and one of the county's railway byways passed into history.

The National Coal Board invested much in the mines in Ayrshire, re-equipping them with modern machinery in an attempt to increase production and make operations more efficient. On the railway aspect, a new locomotive shed was built at Dunaskin in the mid-1960s, replacing the old, cramped locomotive shed. This must be one of the last commercially built steam locomotive sheds in the UK. The Waterside system was always an attraction for enthusiasts, both local and from further afield. The combination of attractive, upland scenery and a rural, steam-worked, industrial railway, linking several mines and a washery, almost 7 miles long, gave endless photographic opportunities.

The Waterside system became even more of an attraction after 1967 (and nationally in 1968) when steam working on the main line came to an end, making the Doon Valley an oasis in a diesel-worked desert. However, the end came in July 1978 under the National Coal Board, when the last deep mines closed and the remaining steam locomotives were retired, and most of the railway was dismantled.

However, this was not the end of rail operations in the Doon Valley. The washery continued in operation for a few more years, with opencast coal coming in by road. A Sentinel shunting locomotive was used, and the Doon Valley branch saw regular, daily coal trains. However, even this ceased in 1986 and the railways in the Doon Valley fell silent – temporarily. The demand for domestic coal had

Cairnhill mine, near Muirkirk; NCB no.21 (Barclay 2284 of 1949) (26 September 1974). JIM DAVIDSON

Laight tip, near Waterside; NCB no.17 (Barclay 1338 of 1917) (8 April 1977).
JIM DAVIDSON

all but dried up, but power stations still had an appetite. There remained rich deposits in the Doon Valley and with huge advances in mechanized excavation techniques, opencast was seen as the way forward. In 1988, a huge opencast mine was started at Chalmerston, between Dunaskin and Dalmellington. The branch line to Waterside was extended to Chalmerston using the trackbed of the old NCB railway, linking up with the section from there to Pennyvenie (which had never been lifted). The coal was extracted and loaded, as dug, straight into HAA two-axle hopper wagons, and taken direct to Killoch Colliery via Falkland Yard, Ayr, for washing and grading. Trains, larger than ever before, were run using modern diesels of class 20, 26, 37, then class 56 and 60, and finally class 66. The line as far as Dunaskin was British Rail property but the newly relaid (ex-NCB) line belonged to Scottish Coal, technically an industrial railway, but worked by main-line trains.

There was another twist to the Doon Valley story: in 1998 another opencast mine was opened at Broomhill, between Patna and Rankinston. To serve this, about a mile of the old line to Belston Junction was relaid and a loop provided at Broomhill for running round. Thus, forty-eight years after

Cairnhill mine, near Muirkirk; NCB no.21 (Barclay 2284 of 1949) (26 September 1974).
JIM DAVIDSON

EWSR 37405 at the Broomhill Opencast Mine opening (11 August 1998).
ARCHIE THOM

BELOW: *EWSR empty coal hoppers propelling towards Broomhill Opencast Mine from Holehouse Junction (18 September 1998).*
MAX FOWLER

EWSR empty coal hoppers loading at Broomhill Opencast Mine (18 September 1998).
MAX FOWLER

closure, Holehouse Junction was recreated. There was even a reopening 'Special' on 11 August 1998, consisting of English, Welsh and Scottish Railways 37405 and an inspection saloon, which ran from the Ayrshire Railway Preservation Group's platform at Dunaskin, down the Doon Valley to the newly reinstated Holehouse Junction to Broomhill.

Unfortunately, geological difficulties were encountered and production ceased in 2002, and the line was lifted in 2004. Production at Chalmerston ceased in Autumn 2010, and the line from Ayr is once again silent.

Waterside was by far the most extensive, but was not the only, industrial railway in Ayrshire. There was a smaller network of industrial lines linking various coal-mines, notably Knockshinnoch and Bank mines, to the north of New Cumnock. These linked in to the main Glasgow and South-Western Main Line to Dumfries and Carlisle at Bank Junction, a half mile to the north of New Cumnock. In the late 1980s, after the closure of the deep mines in the late 1960s, a new coal-processing plant to deal with locally mined opencast coal was built at Knockshinnoch, served by a relaid line from Bank Junction, and worked by main-line locomotives. By 2007, this had been closed and was dismantled in 2008. A branch from the line to Knockshinnoch was revived in 2006 to a new opencast mine at Greenburn; this was still in operation in 2015, again using main-line locomotives.

Garrochburn was a goods-only station located between Kilmarnock and Mauchline, mainly serving the surrounding farming community. From 1925, a branch line, a little over a mile long, ran from here, eastwards to Mauchline colliery. In common with other collieries, a small stud of industrial locomotives was kept to shunt wagons and to take loaded wagons to the exchange sidings at the connection to the main line. Mauchline colliery closed in 1966, along with its branch line.

The Waterside and New Cumnock systems were examples of industrial railways that functioned for 100 years or more, with parts of them being revived due to the continuing demand for coal and becoming part of the main-line system. There were literally dozens of short branch lines from main-line railways serving individual collieries. Indeed, at places like Rankinston (Littlemill Colliey), Murkirk (Kames) and Waterside, freight (almost exclusively coal) kept the respective branch lines open long after passenger trains were withdrawn.

The steelworks in the Glengarnock/Kilbirnie area also had an extensive internal industrial railway system, with the steelworks generating much traffic for BR into the 1980s, when British Steel closed the facility.

Mauchline Colliery; NCB no.16 (Barclay 1116 of 1910) shunting (27 December 1975).
JIM DAVIDSON

Glengarnock Steelworks (1977). JIM DAVIDSON

Eglinton no.6, Eglinton Ironworks, Kilwinning (date unknown). TERRY HARRISON COLLECTION

From the 1840s until 1924, the Eglinton Ironworks in Kilwinning was in operation and was served by a railway striking east from Blacklands Junction on the Byrehill Junction to Dubbs Junction link to the south of Kilwinning. It was extended further east – the 'Doura branch' as far as Perceton, serving up to a dozen coal-mines. The mines did not long survive the closure of the ironworks, and by 1930 the system had passed into history. It is still traceable in parts, some of it along with a couple of overbridges becoming part of a system of paths incorporated into Irvine new town.

There was a small network of industrial railways on the south side of Kilmarnock, off the Riccarton branch, serving the engineering works of Glenfield & Kennedy, Kilmarnock Power Station and the Gas Works, all of which owned their own industrial locos for shunting their sidings. On the north side of the town there was another industrial branch to serve the pottery, manufacturing sanitary ware, of Shanks & Co. at Longpark. The factory closed in 1981, but the branch serving it fell into disuse in the 1960s.

The massive Nobels explosives factory was located at Ardeer, adjacent to Stevenston, on the Ardrossan and Largs branch from the junction at Kilwinning. Exchange sidings were located east of Stevenston Station, and there was a special workers' passenger station within the complex, called 'Ardeer'. Within the works, there was an extensive narrow-gauge system serving the various buildings. As this was a high-security establishment, photographs taken from within the works are very rare. A separate branch, serving the same extensive site, left the main Ayr to Glasgow line at Bogside, north of Irvine, to serve the eastern part of the Nobels site; this was in operation until the mid-1980s and was known as the Snodgrass branch.

Even in the 1980s, a couple of new 'industrial railways' were built. A new paper mill was built at Meadowhead, between Troon and Irvine, completed in 1988. This is served by a short branch line from the Kilmarnock and Troon Railway, with three exchange sidings outside the mill itself. The branch is worked by main-line locomotives, but there is an industrial diesel shunter to work the sidings within the mill. The main traffic handled is a twice-weekly train of china-clay slurry tankers. China clay was originally brought in from Burngullow in Cornwall, using pairs of class 37 locomotives, but now it is imported from Brazil, via Belgium and the Channel Tunnel. The train is worked from Dollands Moor to Irvine, electrically hauled to Mossend Yard, east of Glasgow and diesel-hauled from there to the Caledonian Paper Mill.

Hillhouse Quarry near Troon, a short distance south of the Kilmarnock to Troon railway, is a huge producer of stone, and for decades produced ballast for the main-line railway. A branch line was built from the Shewalton signal box, via exchange sidings, right into the quarry, and ballast trains were a frequent sight in the quarry. With rail privatization, the quality of the stone supplied was deemed not compatible with modern requirements, and the traffic ceased in the mid-1990s.

Further north, at Dalry, part of the old Swinlees colliery branch was revived in the early 1980s to serve a new pharmaceutical factory. It was served by rail daily; however, in mid-2015 there was no rail traffic into or out of the factory.

This is only an overview of the many small and not so small industrial railways that existed at one time or another in Ayrshire. A detailed account of them, their operation and the locomotives would justify a book in its own right.

Hunslet 9092 of 1988 (the last standard gauge diesel shunter built at Hunslet, Leeds) at the Caledonian Mill Exchange Sidings, Irvine (9 September 2010).

Locomotive Manufacturing

Locomotive manufacturing played an important part of the history of the railways in Ayrshire. Andrew Barclay established engineering workshops at the Caledonia works in Kilmarnock in 1840, manufacturing all types of metal products, including winding engines for the rapidly expanding local coal-mining industry. The expanding railway industry was identified as a potential source of work, and the company produced its first steam locomotive in 1859. Barclay's turned out to be a prolific manufacturer of small steam locomotives for heavy industry to work on its railways, and hundreds upon hundreds were produced, in a variety of gauges, for customers throughout the world. Steam locomotive production continued until 1958. In 1927, an order was received from the London, Midland and Scottish Railway (LMS) for a batch of twenty-five 'Fowler 4F' class 0-6-0 tender engines; this was a rare (but not unknown) order from a main-line railway.

In 1876, two employees of Barclay's left and set up a similar company named Grant, Ritchie and

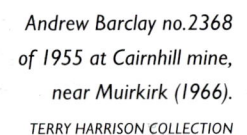

Andrew Barclay no. 2368 of 1955 at Cairnhill mine, near Muirkirk (1966).
TERRY HARRISON COLLECTION

Kilmarnock; LMS class 5MT 'Black 5' 5025 at Barclay's for overhaul (May 1975).
ANDREW ARNOT

138

Aviemore; Andrew Barclay-built loco (no.2017 of 1935) in preservation at the Strathspey Railway (6 June 2007).

Co. elsewhere in Kilmarnock. Like Barclay's, they also built machinery for the mining and other heavy industries. There was fierce competition between the companies. Grant, Ritchie's locomotives were so similar in appearance to Barclay's that it was rumoured that when the two men left Barclay's, they left with bundles of drawings under their arms. Nevertheless, the two companies coexisted for many years, the increased demand brought on by the First World War helping both companies immensely. By the 1920s, the Great Depression had set in and Grant, Ritchie did not survive: the works closed in 1926, liquidation following in 1928 and the name passed into history. There are still some Grant, Ritchie locomotives in preservation.

Back at Barclay's, in 1910, a fireless steam-locomotive design was developed, for use in facilities such as explosives works, munitions depots, paper

Minnivey; preserved Andrew Barclay diesel (no.399 of 1956) ex-Grangemouth Refinery (14 August 1999).

Minnivey; Barclay (no.561 of 1971) (27 June 1999).

mills, oil refineries and similar, where there was a significant fire risk. The fireless locomotive had a receiver rather than a boiler, which was charged with steam from a conventional boiler. The locomotive used that pressurized steam for shunting until the supply was exhausted, whereupon it went to be recharged. The first 'fireless' was completed in 1912, and between then and 1961 a total of 114 was constructed, the last being delivered in 1961. This number was more than every other British manufacturer put together. The locomotives were built on 0-4-0 and 0-6-0 wheel arrangements, with two 'monsters', impressive 0-8-0 locomotives, produced in 1942. Another of Barclay's specialities was the 'crane tank', essentially a small shunting locomotive with a steam-powered crane mounted on it – effectively a mobile crane on rails, very useful in the heavy manufacturing industry, dockyards and so on.

Two notable locomotives were built in 1907 for the Campbeltown and Machrihanish Railway, the only narrow-gauge passenger railway ever built in Scotland. The line, on the Kintyre peninsula, was built to a 2ft 6in gauge and was detached, and miles from, any other railway. The locomotives were of an 0-6-2 wheel arrangement, with side tanks. They worked on the line for its entire life. The railway closed suddenly at the end of the 1931 summer season; these elegant locomotives worked on for the dismantling of the line and when this was complete they were unfortunately scrapped.

Barclay fireless loco (no.1952 of 1928) at Dunaskin (5 July 2015).

During the Second World War, production increased as industries such as coal-mining, iron and steel production, as well as the forces, increased their activity because of the hostilities. Not only locomotives, but also items such as parts for tanks, winches, and so on, as well as other industrial machines, were in demand.

In the 1920s, Barclay's produced a small number of narrow-gauge petrol locomotives, mostly for export, but by the 1930s, it realized that there would be a future in the production of diesel locomotives. The first was produced in 1936 and proved to be a successful venture. Over the next fifty years, diesel locomotives in increasing numbers were produced. The last new steam locomotive was produced in 1956, all new locomotive production thereafter being diesel. A notable order was received from BR in 1957, for a batch of sixteen diesel mechanical shunting locomotives (class 0/1), followed two years later for a further twenty (this became class 06).

In 1948, Barclay's produced their only electric locomotives – under sub-contract for the Metropolitan Vickers Electrical Co. for Dorman Long in Middlesborough. Curiously, they were not allocated numbers in the Company's records, as were all other locomotives built by Barclay's.

With the contraction of the national railway network, and the decrease in heavy industry along with the decline in coal-mining from the early 1960s onwards, there was a corresponding decline in locomotive manufacturing. Barclay's rode out the tide and locomotive production continued, albeit at a smaller volume. When the North British Locomotive Company in Glasgow went into liquidation in 1962 (it did not adapt as well as Barclay's to the transition from steam to diesel traction), Barclay's took over the 'goodwill' from that company. Similarly, Barclay's acquired 'goodwill' from John Fowler & Co. of Leeds in 1968. Andrew Barclay, Sons & Co. ceased to exist as an independent company in August 1972, following a merger with the Hunslet Engine Company of Leeds, the new company being named 'Hunslet–Barclay' in 1989. The move proved to be beneficial for both companies.

Hunslet–Barclay, Kilmarnock; ex-B.R. 20903 'Alison' and 20904 'Janis' (10 September 1990).

Troon; Hunslet–Barclay 20901 and 20904 with a weedkiller train (13 July 1995).

BELOW: *Kilmarnock; BR 143020 at Hunslet–Barclay for refurbishment (27 August 1990).*

At the Caledonia works, production kept going into the 1970s and 1980s. British Rail placed a significant order in June 1984 for twenty-five two-car diesel multiple units (class 143). The bodies were built by the Falkirk firm, Walter Alexander & Co., well known as bus builders, the units being assembled and completed in Kilmarnock. A new railcar shop was built on the site of the old boiler shop. In 1987, Hunslet–Barclay won a further order from British Rail to totally refurbish the forty-strong fleet of class 141 diesel multiple units.

In 1989, Hunslet–Barclay bought seven class 20 diesel electric locomotives from British Rail, gave them an overhaul, and repainted them into an attractive red and two-tone grey livery, for use on two weedkilling trains for use all over the British Rail network. The trains themselves were provided by Chipman and Schering Agrochemicals. The trains ran for five years.

Workload increased, and in view of this, in 1989 it was decided to purchase the former Kilmarnock goods yard, between the existing works and

Kilmarnock; 'Gillian' Barclay (no.6769 of 1990) emerges from the old works and crosses West Langlands Street (27 August 1990).

Kilmarnock Station to the north of West Langlands Street, and to build an entirely new workshop, at a cost of nearly £4 million. This was completed in 1991 and many of the machines were transported across from the old Caledonia works using the rail link. One of the first contracts to be carried out in the new facility was the conversion of most of British Rail's class 155 'Sprinters' to single-car class 153 units. For industry, a large 750hp diesel locomotive was supplied to Blue Circle Industries in 1990, for working their branch line from their cement works in Hope, Derbyshire, to the main Manchester to Sheffield line near Hope Station.

Barclay's survival for so long was due to being able to fulfil small and one-off products for the UK's heavy industry, in a variety of gauges, such as ironworks, steelworks, refineries, paper mills, government establishments and, notably, the coal-mining industry. Over 100 locomotives were exported to countries all over the world. The basic design, both steam and diesel, was simple, rugged and easily maintained. There are very many Barclay's locomotives preserved all over the UK and abroad.

In 2007, Brush Engineering took over Hunslet–Barclay. Then, in 2011, Brush–Barclay were taken over by Wabtec, and 'Barclay's' became Wabtec Rail Scotland. Rail maintenance work continues on the site, and recent work has included the refurbishment of ex-British Rail Mark 3 high-speed train coaches for Great Western Trains, and assembly and refurbishment of container flats.

The old G&SWR's main maintenance works were located at Kilmarnock, in the vee between

Kilmarnock works before takeover and expansion by Brodie Rail (24 April 2010).

Gailes; Class 55 'Deltic' 5502 'Royal Scots Grey' conveying a ScotRail class 334 EMU to Brodie Rail, Kilmarnock for refurbishment (14 June 2013).

the Troon and Dalry lines, north of Kilmarnock Station. After locomotive repairs finished there in the 1960s, it continued in use for the upkeep of track maintenance machines under British Rail. In 2009, a private company, Brodie Rail Engineering, took over the premises, and refurbished and extended the old works. Brodie's, like their neighbour Wabtec Rail Scotland, were in the train maintenance/refurbishment business, and announced their arrival on the scene by winning the contract to refurbish and repaint into Saltire livery ScotRail's forty-strong fleet of class 334 electric multiple units. This took 2½ years and was completed in the summer of 2014. As Kilmarnock is not on the electrified network, the units had to be diesel-hauled from Yoker depot in Clydebank, on the North Clyde line to Kilmarnock.

Brodie Rail engineering, Kilmarnock; Yorkshire Engine Co. no.2676 of 1959 (13 July 2013).

Preservation

During the early 1970s, some local railway enthusiasts realized that Ayrshire's industrial railway heritage was quickly disappearing. Coal-mines were closing at a fast rate, together with the lines and locomotives that moved the output from them. During this period, the two great mines at Killoch, near Ochitree between Ayr and Cumnock, and Barony and its associated power station, near Auchinleck, continued massive production, but the smaller, uneconomic mines were rapidly closing. The National Coal Board's operations at Waterside in the Doon Valley looked particularly vulnerable, so these enthusiasts, anticipating closure of the Waterside system, formed the Ayrshire Railway Preservation Group, with a view to preserving industrial steam in Ayrshire.

A collection of local railway artefacts was gathered, and a temporary base was established at a farm at Fenwick, near Kilmarnock. Because it wasn't near a railway line, it was always considered a temporary home. It was during this period that the Ayrshire Railway Preservation Group acquired their first locomotive – from Cochrane's boiler works in Annan, Dumfriesshire. It is a Ruston Hornsby 0-4-0 diesel mechanical locomotive no 283849 built in 1950, named 'Blinkin' Bess', and was taken to Fenwick in August 1976. Meanwhile, the Group's efforts to find a permanent base for a preservation site continued. Many redundant railway locations were sought in Ayrshire, but none of their requests resulted in success.

In July 1978, the National Coal Board called time on the remaining deep mines in the Doon Valley and those at Pennyvenie and Minnivey, near Dalmellington, were closed, along with what was left of the Waterside system. The washery at Dunaskin was kept going by opencast coal from Benbain, and the railway from Ayr was still in use for coal trains as

Former Scottish Industrial Railway Centre at Minnivey, Dalmellington (3 September 2000).

INDUSTRIAL RAILWAYS AND PRESERVATION

NCB Ayrshire Area no.10 (Andrew Barclay no.2244 of 1947) at the former Scottish Industrial Railway Centre at Minnivey, Dalmellington (22 August 1999). ARCHIE THOM

Scottish Industrial Railway Centre, Minnivey; newly (cosmetic) restored 'Dalmellington Iron Company no.16' (Barclay 1116 of 1910) (27 September 1992).

well. The Ayrshire Railway Preservation Group saw some potential here, and entered into discussions with the National Coal Board for the acquisition of some of the redundant infrastructure. Agreement was reached for a lease on the former Minnivey mine, a drift mine developed in the 1950s with fairly modern buildings that suited the Group admirably. The Group took possession of the site in mid-1980. It was effectively a 'brown field' site, with all the mine gear and railway lines removed, leaving only the buildings and the adjacent 'main line' of the Waterside railway on its way from Dunaskin to Pennyvenie. The fledgling Group nevertheless acquired track and all the paraphernalia that go along with a railway project, and set about the task of making the Minnivey site attractive enough to have paying visitors. There was no comparable attraction within 70 miles of Minnivey. The Group decided to call the new site the 'Scottish Industrial Railway Centre'.

Also in 1980, the Group acquired some of the locomotives that had worked on the Waterside system: no.10, no.19 and no.16 (although no.16 had moved to Barony Colliery) – all Barclay's products, so all locally built. Some rolling stock, mostly coal wagons, had also been assembled. The cavalcade was delivered to Minnivey in mid-1980, and the track from Minnivey down to Dunaskin was lifted. Strangely, the mile and a quarter of track from Minnivey to Pennyvenie was left *in situ*. At the new site, with some track laid, a single engine locomotive shed was built and the site partially landscaped, the Group were sufficiently confident to open the doors to the public. So the first open days were held on 14 and 15 July 1984 and a total of nearly 500 people paid to see what the Group had to offer. Occasional open days were held after that. The Group's next aim was to offer visitors rides behind the locomotive, which was (and still is) NCB Ayrshire area no.10, Barclay no.2244 built in 1947. This locomotive was built by Barclay's for the NCB.

The Group also possess what is believed to be the only working fireless locomotive in the United Kingdom. Built by Barclay's in Kilmarnock in 1928 (works number 1952), it worked at the Shell Refinery at Ardrossan until closure in 1986, thus becoming the last commercially operated steam locomotive in Scotland. Shell donated the historic locomotive to the Group, in full working order, and it has been maintained and exhibited as such since then. It had a period as a static exhibit, but a long and meticulous overhaul returned it to working order in the summer of 2015.

Minnivey; the only main-line train ever to reach the former Scottish Industrial Railway Centre; 37043 and 37212 with a Branch Line Society railtour (24 August 1996).
ARCHIE THOM

Platform scene at the relocated Scottish Industrial Railway Centre at Dunaskin NCB Ayrshire Area No. 10 (Barclay 2244 of 1947) present (7 July 2013).

The underframe of an ex-LMS brake van (damaged by fire during its original restoration) was used, and a passenger carrying van was built. A section of the main line was used for brake van rides. This was gradually upgraded, and eventually renewed with fresh ballast, with a proper passenger platform and loop. By the early 1990s, around 2,000 to 3,000 visitors a season were at-tracted to Minnivey over a dozen open days during each summer. The aim was to run a passenger service from Minnivey over the 2 miles, through the Chalmerston opencast mine, to Dunaskin. Two British Rail Mk 2 carriages were obtained, platforms were built at both locations, but difficulties with Scottish Coal and Railtrack meant that it never came to pass.

The Group, in arrangement with the Dalmellington and District Conservation Trust (who had opened an open-air industrial museum at Dunaskin), had use of the National Coal Board locomotive shed at Dunaskin, as well as the adjacent Wagon Shop. Many of the Group's growing collection of industrial steam and vintage diesel locomotives were stored here, out of public view. In 2002, in association with the Trust, after twenty-two years,

NCB no.10 (Barclay no.2244 of 1947) in action at the relocated Scottish Industrial Railway Centre, Dunaskin (14 July 2013).

Sentinal (no.10012 built 1959) with restored goods wagons at SIRC, Dunaskin (26 May 2013).

the Group decided to relocate its operations from Minnivey to Dunaskin.

This was almost a case of starting again. Whilst the facilities were much better and a passenger platform had already been built, there was much upgrading of existing track and a running line to be built. The running line was laid and passed for passenger running. By 2007, the newly relocated Scottish Industrial Railway Centre was ready to receive visitors again. Since then, the old Dalmellington Iron Company's Engineers' Shop has been adapted to become an industrial and railway museum, the shop has been upgraded and a café has been created. The large museum includes photographic displays, and industrial and railway exhibits portraying the county's rich industrial heritage. There is also a G-gauge, live, steam model railway in the museum. The facilities provided for the visitor equal those of much larger railway preservation sites.

The Scottish Industrial Railway Centre at Dunaskin

NCB no.10 (Barclay no.224 of 1947) alongside fireless loco (Barclay no.1952 of 1928) at Dunaskin (5 July 2015).

Newly restored fireless loco (Barclay no.1952 of 1928) at Dunaskin (5 July 2015).

has become a steam centre and a living museum, where visitors can get a glimpse of Ayrshire's industrial past and enjoy a steam-hauled brake van ride, where industrial steam and vintage diesel locomotives can be seen at work in an authentic setting. Generally, the Centre is open during public holidays from Easter onwards, and every Sunday throughout July and August.

Ex-NCB loco shed at Scottish Industrial Railway Centre, Dunaskin (14 July 2013).

APPENDIX I

Ayrshire's Railway Stations: Opening and Closure Dates

	Opened	Closed to goods	Closed to passengers	
Alloway	17 May 1906	7 December 1959	1 December 1930	
Annbank	1 September 1870	6 July 1964	10 September 1951	
Ardrossan Town	28 July 1834	3 April 1972	1 January 1968	
Ardrossan Town	19 January 1987		Open	Reopened
Ardrossan Winton Pier	28 July 1840		1 January 1968	
Ardrossan Harbour	19 January 1987		Open	
Ardrossan Montgomerie Pier	4 September 1888		18 April 1966	
Ardrossan South Beach	1 January 1883		Open	
Auchenmade	4 September 1888		4 July 1932	
Auchincruive	?? March 1871	5 October 1964	10 September 1951	
Auchinleck	9 August 1848		6 December 1965	
Auchinleck	14 May 1984		Open	Reopened
Ayr				
Ayr (new)			Open	
Northside	5 August 1839	30 August 1971	1 July 1857	
Harbour – North Quay	12 August 1840	??		
Cattle Market	??	1 March 1965		
Harbour – South Quay		?? 1957		
Harbour – Texaco siding		31 December 1973		
Balchriston	17 May 1906	28 February 1955	1 December 1930	
Barassie	?? June 1859	6 July 1964	Open	

AYRSHIRE'S RAILWAY STATIONS: OPENING AND CLOSURE DATES

	Opened	Closed to goods	Closed to passengers	
Barleith	?? June 1907	N.A.	6 April 1964	
Barrhill	5 October 1877	6 April 1964	Open	
Barrmill	26 June 1873	5 November 1962	5 November 1962	
Beith North	21 July 1870	28 October 1963	4 June 1951	
Beith Town	26 June 1873	5 October 1954	5 November 1962	
Bogside	23 March 1840	N.A.	2 January 1967	
Cairntable Halt	24 September 1928	N.A.	3 April 1950	
Cassillis	13 October 1856	3 October 1960	1 December 1954	
Catrine	1 September 1903	6 July 1964	3 May 1943	
Commondyke	1 October 1897	N.A.	7 July 1950	
Cronberry	1 July 1872	2 March 1964	10 September 1951	
Crosshill	24 May 1860	N.A.	1 March 1862	
Crosshouse	1 September 1872	6 July 1964	18 April 1966	
Cumnock	20 May 1850	7 September 1964	6 December 1965	
Cumnock (A&C)	1 July 1872	1 July 1959	10 September 1951	
Cunninghamhead	4 April 1843	1 February 1960	1 January 1951	
Dailly	24 May 1860	6 April 1964	6 September 1965	
Dalmellington	7 August 1856	6 July 1964	6 April 1964	
Dalry	21 July 1840	3 May 1965	Open	
Dalry Junction	?? November 1859	N.A.	31 December 1859	
Dalrymple	1 November 1856	6 April 1964	1 December 1954	
Dalrymple Junction (goods only)		6 April 1964		
Darvel	1 June 1896	6 July 1964	6 April 1964	
Dipple (goods only)	17 May 1906	28 February 1955		
Dreghorn	22 May 1848	6 July 1964	6 April 1964	
Drongan	1 March 1876	6 July 1964	10 September 1951	
Drybridge	?? 1818	2 November 1959	3 March 1969	
Dumfries House	1 July 1872	N.A.	13 June 1949	
Dunlop	27 March 1871	7 September 1964	7 November 1966	
Dunlop	5 June 1967	N.A.	Open	Reopened
Dunure	17 May 1906	28 February 1955	1 December 1930	
Fairlie (High)	1 June 1880	1 May 1961	Open	
Fairlie Pier	1 July 1872	5 October 1954	1 October 1971	
Gailes	1 June 1893	N.A.	2 January 1967	
Galston	9 August 1848	6 July 1964	6 April 1964	
Garrochburn (goods only)	??	4 October 1965		
Giffen	4 September 1888		4 July 1932	
Girvan (Old)	24 May 1860	??	1 April 1893	
Girvan	5 October 1877	N.A.	Open	
Gatehead	?? 1818	7 September 1964	3 March 1969	
Glengarnock	21 July 1840	4 January 1965	Open	
Glengarnock High	1 December 1889	c. 1945	2 December 1930	

152

AYRSHIRE'S RAILWAY STATIONS: OPENING AND CLOSURE DATES

	Opened	Closed to goods	Closed to passengers	
Glenside	17 May 1906	28 February 1955	1 December 1930	
Grangeton (goods only)		28 February 1955		
Grangeston Halt	?? 1941	N.A.	6 September 1965	
Gree (goods only)	1 May 1903	?? 1950		
Greenan Castle (goods only)	17 May 1906	7 December 1959		
Heads of Ayr (1st)	17 May 1906	7 December 1959	1 December 1930	
Heads of Ayr (2nd)	17 May 1947	N.A.	16 September 1968	
Holehouse Junction	?? June 1904	N.A.	3 April 1950	
Hollybush	7 August 1856	1 February 1960	6 April 1964	
Hurlford	9 August 1848	6 July 1964	7 March 1955	
Hurlford Mineral Sidings (goods only)	??	24 January 1966		
Irvine	5 August 1839	N.A.	Open	
Irvine Bank Street	2 June 1890	30 December 1939	28 July 1930	
Irvine Harbour (goods only)	11 January 1841	26 August 1970		
Kilbirnie	1 June 1905	3 May 1965	27 June 1966	
Kilbirnie South	1 December 1889	2 December 1930	2 December 1930	
Kilkerran	24 May 1860	2 March 1964	6 September 1965	
Killochan	24 May 1860	7 December 1959	1 January 1951	
Kilmarnock	4 April 1843	N.A.	Open	
Kilmarnock (goods only)		3 September 1969		
St Marnock	1 March 1847	May 1983		
Kilmaurs	26 June 1873	7 September 1964	7 November 1966	
Kilmaurs	12 May 1984	N.A.	Open	Reopened
Kilwinning	23 March 1840		Open	
Kilwinning East	4 September 1888	?? 1951	4 July 1932	
Knoweside	17 May 1906	28 February 1955	1 December 1930	
Largs	1 June 1885	25 September 1967	Open	
Lissens (goods only)	4 September 1888	17 December 1950		
Lochside	12 August 1840	4 July 1955	4 July 1955	
Lochside (now Lochwinnoch)	27 June 1966		Open	Reopened
Lochwinnoch	1 June 1906	8 September 1969	27 June 1966	
Loudounhill	1 May 1905	11 September 1939	25 September 1939	
Lugar	?? January 1860	5 October 1964	3 July 1950	
Lugton	27 March 1871	5 October 1964	7 November 1966	
Lugton High	1 June 1903		4 July 1932	
Maidens	17 May 1906	28 February 1955	1 December 1930	

AYRSHIRE'S RAILWAY STATIONS: OPENING AND CLOSURE DATES

	Opened	Closed to goods	Closed to passengers	
Mauchline	9 August 1848	1 November 1965	6 December 1965	
Maybole (1st)	13 October 1856	5 April 1965	24 May 1860	
Maybole	24 May 1860	N.A.	Open	
Monkton	5 August 1839	3 May 1960	29 October 1940	
Montgreenan	1 February 1878	5 October 1959	7 March 1955	
Muirkirk (Old)	9 August 1848		c. 1896	
Muirkirk	c. 1896	7 September 1964	5 October 1964	
New Cumnock	20 May 1850	7 September 1964	6 December 1965	
New Cumnock	27 May 1991	N.A.	Open	Reopened
Newmilns	28 May 1850	6 July 1964	6 April 1964	
Newtonhead	1 October 1864	N.A.	1 April 1868	
Newton on Ayr	1 November 1886	N.A.	Open	
Ochiltree	1 July 1872	6 January 1964	10 September 1951	
Patna (Old)	7 August 1856		c. 1897	
Patna (New)	c. 1887	6 July 1964	6 April 1964	
Prestwick Town	5 August 1839	7 September 1964	Open	
Prestwick Airport	5 September 1994	N.A.	Open	
Rankinston	1 January 1884	2 November 1959	3 April 1950	
Riccarton and Craigie (goods only)		5 July 1965		
Riccarton – Glenfield and Kennedy	31 March 1971			
Saltcoats (1st)	27 July 1840		1 July 1858	
Saltcoats (2nd)	1 July 1858		?? 1882	
Saltcoats (3rd)	?? 1882	5 April 1965	Open	
Saltcoats North	4 September 1888		4 July 1932	
Skares	1 July 1901	6 January 1964	10 September 1951	
Springside	1 June 1890	N.A.	6 April 1964	
Stevenston	27 July 1840	5 October 1964	Open	
Stevenston Moorpark	4 September 1888		4 July 1932	
Stewarton	27 March 1871	5 October 1964	7 November 1966	
Stewarton	5 June 1967	N.A.	Open	Reopened
Tarbolton	1 September 1870	6 January 1964	4 January 1943	
Trabboch	1 July 1896	N.A.	10 September 1951	
Troon (Old)	5 August 1848	6 July 1964	2 May 1892	
Troon	2 May 1892	N.A.	Open	
Troon Templehill (goods only)	1 November 1965	N.A.		
Troon Harbour		3 December 1973	N.A.	
Turnberry	17 September 1906	28 February 1955	2 March 1942	
Waterside	7 August 1856	6 July 1964	6 April 1964	
West Kilbride	1st May 1878	5 October 1964	Open	

APPENDIX II

Railway Abbreviations

A&C	Ayr and Cumnock Railway
CR	Caledonian Railway
DBS	DB Schenker
EWSR	English, Welsh and Scottish Railway
FHH	Freightliner Heavy Haul
G&SWR	Glasgow and South-Western Railway
GBRf	GB Railfreight
GGPTE	Greater Glasgow Passenger Transport Executive
K&TR	Kilmarnock and Troon Railway
LMS	London, Midland and Scottish Railway
Route miles	*see* Track miles
SPTE	Strathclyde Passenger Transport Executive

Track miles (as opposed to route miles) the actual length of railway track. For example, if Kilmarnock to Troon is 8 route miles, with double track it would be 16 miles. Track miles also includes loops and sidings.

Bibliography

The following books were invaluable as sources of reference in compiling this book, all of which are recommended for reading about the railways of Ayrshire and the south-west of Scotland.

Alexander, F. and Nicholl, E. S., *The Register of Scottish Signal Boxes* (Signalling Record Society, 1990)

Broad, H., *Rails to Ayr* (Ayrshire Archaelogical and Natural History Society, 1989)

Hawkins, C., Reeve, G. and Stevenson, J., *L.M.S. Engine Sheds Volume 7 The Glasgow and South-Western Railway* (Irwell Press, 1990)

Lindsay, D. M. E., *The Glasgow and South-Western Railway – Register of Stations, Routes and Lines* (Glasgow and South-Western Railway Association, 2002)

Nock, O. S., *The Caledonian Railway* (Ian Allan, 1964)

Ross, D., *The Glasgow and South-Western Railway: a History* (Stenlake Publishing, 2014)

Smith, D. L., *The Dalmellington Iron Company, Its Engines and Men* (David & Charles, 1967)

The Stephenson Locomotive Society, *The Glasgow and South-Western Railway* (The Stephenson Locomotive Society, 1950)

Thomas, J. (revised J.S. Paterson) *A Regional History of the Railways of Great Britain – Volume 6 Scotland, The Lowlands and Borders* (David & Charles, 1984)

Wear, R., *Barclay 150: 1840–1990* (1990) (Hunslet-Barclay Ltd, Kilmarnock, 1990)

Wham, A., *Ayrshire's Forgotten Railways: a Walker's Guide* (Oakwood Press, 2013)

Various magazine articles and publications from the Glasgow and South-Western Railway Association.

Various Timetables from Bradshaws, the London, Midland and Scottish Railway, British Railway and ScotRail.

Websites:
www.arpg.or.uk
www.scottishindustrialrailwaycentre.org.uk
www.gswrr.co.uk

Index

Note: photographs shown in *italics*

Abellio 109, 119
Accident, Barassie Junction 55, 56
Ailsa Hospital 35
Airdrie 109
Allloway Junction 62, 68, 85, 99
Alloway 62, 68, *69*, *73*, 73, 128
Alloway Tunnel 61
Alstom 108
Amey Roadstone 109
Andrew Barclay, Sons & Co. 30, 130, *138*, *138*, 139, 140, 141
Annan 27, 119
Annbank 9, 38, *41*, 52, 72, *73*
Annbank Junction 39, *40*, 41, 42, 49, 56, 59, 67, 69, 70, 98, *100*, *103*, *104*, 112, 121
Annick Water (Stewarton) Viaduct *49*, 49
Ardeer 67, 71, 136, 137
Ardrossan 8, 19, 21, 44, 46, 47, 50, 66, 70, 83, 89, 119, 128
Ardrossan Harbour 14, 46, 83, 90, 91, 128
Ardrossan Montgomerie Pier 46, 66, 67
Ardrossan North 46, 67, *68*
Ardrossan South Beach *20*, 91
Ardrossan Town 91, 128
Ardrossan Winton Pier 91
Auchencruive 9, 38
Auchenmade 46, 67, 68
Auchinleck *21*, *22*, 22, *24*, 27, *27*, 41, 42, 43, 70, 73, *84*, 84, 96, *97*, 98, 119, 128, 145
Auldgirth 27
Auldhouseburn Junction 43
Aviemore 139
Ayr 8, 9, 31, 38, 41, 46, 47, 52, 56, 59, 60, 67, 68, 69, 70, 71, 73, 74, *76*, 77, 78, 80, 83, 84, *88*, 89, 90, *91*, 91, *92*, 94, *105*, *106*, 112, 119, 124, 126, 130

Ayr & Cumnock Railway (A&C) 38, 49, 51, 72, 73, 98
Ayr & Dalmellington Railway 31
Ayr & Galloway Railway 29
Ayr (Northside) (Old) *17*, *18*, 32
Ayr (Townhead) (New) *18*, 32
Ayr County Council 85
Ayr Engine Shed (Depot) 38, *77*, *81*, *82*, 83, 110, *111*, *112*, 115
Ayr Harbour 9, 30, *121*
Ayr Hospital 128
Ayr Texaco
Ayrshire Electrification Project 90
Ayrshire Railway Preservation Group 97, 135, 145, 147

Balchriston 62, 68, 73
Ballantrae 35
Ballochmyle Viaduct *26*, *47*, 48
Bank Junction 101, 135
Bank Mine 135
Barassie *12*, *13*, 13, 14, *16*, 52, *64*, 85, 119, 121
Barassie C&W Works 64
Barassie Junction *53*, 85, 86, 90, 100, 112
Barleith Halt 63, 71, 74
Barony Colliery 145
Barrhead 36, 37, 46, 68, 83, 86, 116, 119, 123, 126
Barrhill *35*, 35, 116, *117*, 126
Barrmill 46, 74
Bathgate 109
Beattock 23, 122, 124
Beeching, Dr Richard 83
Beeching Report 74, 86, 94, 96, 98, 128
Beith 37, 46, 124
Beith North 14, 74
Beith Town 74
Belgium 101, 123
Belston Junction 41, 42, 50, 51, 52, 67, 72, 73, 133

Benbain Opencast 145
Blackhouse Junction 38, *112*
Blacklands Junction 20, 136
Blue Circle Industries 143
BMK Carpets 7
Bogside 14, 137
Bowhouse *24*, *120*
Brackenhill Junction 27, 60, 68
Brazil 101, 123
British & Irish Grand Junction Railway 29
British Rail 64, 106, 116, 143, 144
British Rail 85, 86, 89, 104, 125, 142, 143
British Rail Engineering Ltd 91
British Railways 60, 71, 74, 83, 98, 103
British Steel Corporation 99, 135
Brodick 44
Brodie Rail Engineering *144*, 144
Broomhill *52*, 133, *134*, 135
Brownhill Junction 60
Brush-Barclay 143
Burngullow (Cornwall) 101, 137
Burnockhill 42
Burnockhill Viaduct 49
Burns, Robert 8
Burnton Viaduct (Dalrymple) *29*, 48
Butlin, Sir Billy 69
Butlin's Holiday Camp, Ayr 69, 73, 85
Byrehill Junction 20, 22, *105*, 136
Byres 19

Cairnhill Mine 42, 73, 99, *132*, 138
Cairnryan 7, 109
Cairntable Halt 67, 71
Caldwell 37
Caledonia Works, Kilmarnock 138, 142
Caledonian Paper Mill (Irvine) *100*, 101, 123, 137, *137*
Caledonian Railway 36, 37, 42, 43, 46, 47, 56, 62, 65, 124, 128

157

INDEX

Campbeltown & Machriehanish Railway 140
Cardiff 7
Carlisle 23, 38, 60, 63, 83, 86, 94, 98, 119, 124
Carronbridge 27
Cart Junction 60
Cassillis 32, 74
Castle Douglas 29
Cathcart 46, 66
Catrine 57, *58*, *59*, 59, *60*, 60, 68, 69, 99
Challoch Junction 35
Chalmerston 110, 114, 115, 121, 133, 135, 148
Channel Tunnel 109, 137
Chipman & Schering 142
Closeburn 24, 27
Clyde Port Authority 99
Coalburn 43
Cochrane Mill 14
Colas Railfreight 109, 115, 123
Commondyke 22
Compass Railtours 125
Corkerhill 46
Corton 29
Coventry 7
Coylton 131
Cronberry 22, 41, 42, 72, 73, 99
Crookston 97
Crosshill
Crosshouse 21, *21*, *128*, 128
Crowbandsgate 110, *112*, 112, *113*, 115, 116, 121
Culzean Castle 60
Cummertrees 27
Cumnock 27, 38, 41, 42, 48, 49, 51, 73, 84
Cumnock (A&C) 70, 73
Cunninghamhead 20, *21*, 74, 81
Currock 46

Dailly 33
Dalmellington 29, 31, 33, 41, 51, 67, 71, 72, 83, 114, 121, 129, 131, 133
Dalmellington & District Conservation Trust 148
Dalmellington Iron Company 30, 129, 149
Dalry 14, *14*, 20, 24, 37, 46, 60, 86, 114, 116, 124, 128, 137
Dalry & North Johnstone Railway 60
Dalry Junction
Dalrymple 31, 32, 49, 74
Dalrymple (Burnton) Viaduct *29*, 131
Dalrymple Junction 29, 32, 115
Dalston 126
Darvel 22, 57, 63, 69, 71, 74, 83
Daventry 126
DB Schenker 109, 115, 117, 123
Derbyshire 115
Diesel Multiple Units
  BR class 101 *12*, *15*, *90*, 90
  BR class 107 *10*, 11, *15*, *88*, *90*, 90
  BR class 108 87
  BR class 120 88
  BR class 126 *12*, *16*, *33*, 74, 79, 80, 80, 85, 90
  BR class 141 95
  BR class 144 *142*

BR class 155 143
BR class 155 143
BR class 156 *13*, *17*, *27*, *34*, *35*, *37*, *92*, *94*, 94, 97, 106, *107*, *118*, 119, *120*
BR Inter City 125 *15*, *111*, 126, *127*
Diesel railbus: BR Wickham *128*
Dipple Goods 62, 73
Direct Rail Systems 12
Dollands Moor 123, 137
Doon Valley 29, 30, 114, 121, 129, 130, 132, 133, 135, 145
Doon Viaduct 61
Dornock 27
Doura 20, 136
Dreghorn 21, 128
Drongan 41, 42, 51, 52, 72, 73, 99
Drumclog 56, 69
Drumdow 42
Drybridge 11, *11*, 13, 85, 86
Dubbs Junction 20, 22, 136
Dumfries 23, 24, 27, 35, 38, 41, 56, 59, 60, 63, 83, 86, 98, 119, 122, 126
Dumfries House 41, 42, 74
Dumfries-shire 7, 98
Dunaskin 30, 129, *130*, 130, *131*, 132, 140, 147, *148*, 148, *149*, 149, *150*, 150
Dunlop *37*, 37, 84, 96, 116, *118*, 126, 133
Dunlop, John 8
Dunragit 35
Dunure 8, 60, *62*, 62, 68, 73
Dutch National Railways 109
Dykes Junction 42, 73
Dykes Viaduct *48*, 49

East Ayrshire 7
East Kilbride 120
Edinburgh 43, 69, 109
Edinburgh Waverley 80
Eglinton Ironworks 20, *136*, 136
Elderslie 60
Electric Multiple Units
  BR class 303 *106*
  BR class 318 *19*, *43*, *45*, *91*, 91, *92*, 93, 93
  BR class 334 *44*, *93*, *107*, 108, 144
  BR class 380 *2*, *44*, *107*, 109, 119, *120*
Electro Motive Diesel 109, 110
English, Welsh & Scottish Railway 109, 110, 115, 123, 135
Enterkine viaduct *41*, 49

Fairlie 8
Fairlie (High) *44*, 44, 91, 121
Fairlie Pier 44, 70
Fairlie Pier Junction *44*, 44
Falkirk High 80
Falkland Junction *75*, 76
Falkland Yard 35, 115, 133
Fenwick 145
Fiddlers' Ferry Power Station 122
Fireless locomotive *140*, 140, 147
First Group 106, 108
First World War 65
Fort William 124
Foster Yeoman 109
Freightliner 109, 110, 115

Gailes 14, *16*, *144*
Galston 22, 56
Garleffan Opencast 112
Garnock Viaduct *50*, 50
Garrochburn 135
Gasswater 22, 42
Gatehead *10*, 11, 13, 57, 85, 86, 116
GB Railfreight 109
General Motors 109, 110
German Railways 109
Giffen 46, *66*, *67*, 67, 68, 104, 116, 117, 124
Giffen Junction 66
Girvan 8, 29, 33, 34, 35, 59, 60, 68, 71, 73, 80, 86, 94, 109, 116, *117*, 119, 124, 126
Girvan & Portpatrick Junction Railway 35, 36
Glaisnock Viaduct 48, 49
Glasgow 7, 23, 38, 43, 56, 60, 66, 69, 109, 137
Glasgow & South Western Main Line 119, 122, 124, 125, 126, 135
Glasgow & South Western Railway 13, 29, 31, 36, 43, 46, 47, 51, 56, 59, 60, 63, 65, 66, 68, 71, 83, 121, 130, 131, 143
Glasgow Airport 109
Glasgow Central 43, 46, 47, 66, 85, 86, 90, 93, 94, 97, 108
Glasgow Queen Street 43, 80
Glasgow St Enoch 14, 37, 44, 46, 63, 80, 83, 84
Glasgow, Barrhead & Kilmarnock Joint Railway 36, 46, 49
Glasgow, Barrhead & Neilston Railway 36
Glasgow, Dumfries & Carlisle Railway 24, 29
Glasgow, Paisley, Kilmarnock & Ayr Railway 13, 14, 24, 29
Glenbuck 43, *70*
Glenburn 123
Gleneagles 62
Glenfield & Kennedy 7, 136
Glengall Junction 35
Glengarnock 7, 14, *14*, 135, 135
Glengarnock High
Glenside *62*, 62, 68, 73
Glenwhilly 35
Gourock 108
Grange 116
Grangemouth 103, 115, 117, 122, 123, 126
Grangeton 62, 73
Grangeton Halt 62
Grant, Richie & Co. 138, 139
Great Britain Railfreight (GBRf) 110
Great Cumbrae 7
Great Western Trains 143
Greater Glasgow Passenger Transport Executive 89
Gree Goods 68
Gree Viaduct *50*, 50
Greenan Castle Goods 62, 73
Greenburn *114*, 114, 115, *127*, 135
Greenock 46, 116
Gretna Green 27, 98, 119
Gretna Junction 24, 27

158

INDEX

Hamilton 56
Hargreaves 121
Hawkhill Junction *38*, 38, 78
Heads of Ayr *61*, 62, 68, 69, 73
Heads of Ayr (2nd) 69, 73, 85
Heathfield *38*, *39*
Helensburgh 109, 124
Highland Railway 65
Hillhouse Quarry 10, 137
Hindsward Pit 42
Holehouse Junction *31*, 41, 42, 50, 51, *51*, 52, 67, 71, 72, 73, 135
Hollybush *30*, *31*, 31, 51
Holywood 27
Hope, Derbyshire 143
Houldsworth Mine 30, 129
Howwood 14
Hunslet Barclay *141*, 141, *142*, 142, *143*
Hunslet Engine Co. 141
Hunter, Sir Tom 8
Hunterston B Power Station 122
Hunterston Junction 93
Hunterston Port 91, *99*, *100*, 100, 110, 115, 121, 122
Hurlford 22, 27, 63, *64*, 74, 116, 126
Hurlford Junction 56
Hurlford Mineral Sidings 63
Hurlford Shed 63, 83

Inverness 124
Ireland 109
Irvine 8, 14, *15*, 21, 22, 46, 47, *64*, 64, 66, 83, 116, 119, *120*, 128, 136, 137
Irvine Bank Street 47, 67
Irvine Harbour
Irvine S&T Works 64
Isle of Arran 7, 44, 46, 83
Isle of Man 66

John Fowler & Co. 141
Johnstone 14
Johnstone North 60

Kames Mine 70, 99, 135
Kay Park Junction 57, 116
Kilbarchan 60, 128
Kilbirnie 46, 60, 66, 128, 135
Kilbirnie South 67
Kilkerran *33*, 33, *107*, *116*, 116, 126
Killoch Colliery *41*, 72, 73, 99, 101, *110*, 110, 114, 115, 121, 133, 145
Killochan *33*, 33
Kilmarnock 9, 20, 21, 22, 23, 24, 27, 36, 38, 41, 46, 47, 56, 57, 59, 63, 68, 69, *75*, *80*, 83, 84, 85, *86*, 86, 87, *88*, *89*, 89, *90*, 92, *94*, 94, 97, 98, 103, *104*, *107*, 114, 116, 119, *123*, 126, 135, *136*, 138, *138*, 141, *142*, 142, *143*, 144
Kilmarnock & Troon Railway 9, 14, 57, 100, 112, 119, 121, 123, 137
Kilmarnock (Long Lyes) 113
Kilmarnock Goods
Kilmarnock Open Day 94, *95*, *96*
Kilmarnock Power Station 57, 136
Kilmaurs 37, 84, 85, 96, 97, 119
Kilwinning 14, *15*, 19, 46, 47, 50, 66, 90, 9, 116
Kilwinning East 46, 67, *67*, 68
Kirkconnel 27, 98, 119, 121

Knockshinnoch *101*, *103*, 110, 114, 116, 135
Knoweside 62, 68, 73
Kyle of Lochalsh 125

Laigh Milton Viaduct 11, *11*, *13*
Laight Tip 133
Lanark 43, 70, 73, 83
Lanarkshire 7
Lanarkshire & Ayrshire Railway 46, 47, 50, 67, 103, 124
Largs 8, 44, *45*, 66, 89, 90, 91, *93*, 93, 99, 115, 116, 119
Largs accident 91
Lissens Goods 67, 68
Little Cumbrae 7
Littlemill Colliery 50, 52, 73, 135
Llandudno 97
Loadhaul 109
Lochridge 116
Locomotives, industrial:
Diesel:
Andrew Barclay 399/1956 *139*
Andrew Barclay 6769/1990 *143*
Andrew Barclay 561/1971 *140*
Hunslet Engine Co. 9092/1988 *137*
Sentinel 10012/1959 *149*
Yorkshire Engine Co. 2676/1959 *145*
Steam:
Andrew Barclay 1116/1910 *135*, *146*
Andrew Barclay 1338/1917 *129*
Andrew Barclay 1614/1918 *130*
Andrew Barclay 1952/1928 (fireless) *140*, *149*, *150*
Andrew Barclay 2017/1935 *139*
Andrew Barclay 2244/1947 *95*, *145*, *146*, *147*, *148*, *149*, *150*
Andrew Barclay 2284/1949 *132*
Andrew Barclay 2335/ 1953 *130*
Andrew Barclay 2368/1955 *138*
Locomotives, main line:-
Diesel:
BR class 08 *64*, *73*, 115
EWSR class 08 *113*
BR class 20 *21*, *27*, *45*, *64*, 72, 79, *81*, *101*, 109, 133
Hunslet Barclay class 20 *141*, *142*, 142
BR class 24 77
BR class 25 72, *82*, 89
BR class 26 *16*, *31*, *53*, 72, *102*, *104*, 133
BR class 27 *38*, 72, *81*, *82*
BR class 31 *105*, 126, *127*
BR class 37 *18*, *29*, *30*, *31*, *40*, *41*, *42*, *54*, *96*, 99, *101*, *102*, *103*, *105*, 109, *110*, 125, 126, 133, 135, 137, *147*
BR class 40 *45*, 77, *77*, 78
BR class 45 *24*, *26*, 77, *86*, 87
BR class 47 *11*, *25*, 28, *32*, *54*, 78, *88*, *89*, 109, 125
BR class 50 *87*, *104*
BR class 55 *143*
BR class 56 *11*, *39*, 99, *100*, *103*, 109
BR Class 58 109
BR class 60 *15*, *16*, *32*, 99, *99*, 109, *111*, 133
Colas class 56 *55*, 115, *123*, 125, 133
Colas class 66 *115*

DB Schenker class 66 *96*, *97*, 117, *122*, 123, *125*
DRS class 37 *57*, *122*
DRS class 66 *125*
EWS class 66 *12*, *53*, *64*, 110, *111*, *112*, *113*, *114*, 133
Freightliner class 66 *27*, *54*, *98*, *101*, *112*, *121*, *123*
GBRf *113*
National Power class 59 *109*
Virgin class 57 *24*, *28*
Steam:
BR 'Standards' 72
BR 'Standard' 4MT *70*, *75*, *76*
BR 'Standard' 5MT *9*, *38*
BR 'Clan' *17*, *22*
Caledonian 'Jumbo' Goods *55*, *63*, *69*, *72*
G & SWR Railmotor *58*
Highland Railway 'Jones' Goods *22*
LMS class 4MT 60
LMS 'Black 5' *18*, *25*, *29*, *34*, *39*, *40*, 60, *63*, *64*, *72*, *95*, *124*, *138*
LMS class 2P 60, 72
LMS Fairburn 4MT *58*, *73*, *75*
LMS Fowler 4F *138*
LMS Hughes mogul 'Crab' *14*, *72*
LMS 'Jubilee' *17*
LMS 'Princess' *23*
LNER class A1 *53*
LNER class A3 *81*
LNER class A4 *124*
LNER class B1 *60*, *75*, *76*
LNER class K4 *40*, *125*
Lochgreen Junction 52, *54*, *55*, 79, 91, *123*, *127*
Lochside 14, 74, *96*, 128
Lochwinnoch 60, 66, 74, *96*, 96, 128
Logan Junction 42
London & South Western Railway 59
London Euston 63, 86, 96
London St Pancras 37
London, Midland & Scottish Railway 65, 70, 71, 74, 138, 148
Longannet Power Station 122
Longpark (Kilmarnock) 136
Loudounhill 56, 69
Lugar 22
Lugar Ironworks 22
Lugar Water Viaduct 48
Lugton 37, 37, 46, 50, 68, 74, 84, 86, 116, 117, 124, 126
Lugton High 46, 67

Maidens 60, 62, 68, 73
Maidens & Dunure Light Railway 60, *61*, *63*, 68, 69, 73, 85, 128, *128*
Mainline 109
Mallaig 124
Manson steam railmotor 59
Marquis of Ailsa 62
Martnaham Loch 131
Massey Ferguson 7
Mauchline *25*, *26*, 27, 38, 41, 47, 59, 69, 70, 73, 83, *84*, 86, 99, *101*, *112*, 116, *114*, *117*, 124, 126, 128, 135
Mauchline Colliery *135*, 135
Maybole *32*, *32*, 33, 74, 116, 119
Maybole (Old)

159

INDEX

Mayfield Junction   57
Meadowhead (Caledonian Paper Mill, Irvine)   100, *101*, 137
Meadowhead Mine   131, 132
Metropolitan Cammell   94, 108
Metropolitan Vickers   141
Mid Lanarkshire Lines   43
Minnivey   *139*, 140, *145*, 145, *146*, 147, 148, 149
Monkton   14, *17*, 56, *69*, 69, 115, 123
Monkton Junction   98
Montgreenan   *20*, 20, 74
Morecambe   86
Mossblown   38
Mossblown Junction   39, 56, 123
Mossend   126, 137
Mossgiel Tunnel   *25*, 48
Motherwell   23, 99
Muirend   46
Muirkirk   22, 38, 41, 42, 43, 46, 47, 48, 51, 69, 70, *71*, 73, 83, 99, 135

National Coal Board   131, 132, 145, 147, 148
National Express   106, 108
National Power   109
Neilston   37, 46, 66
Network Rail   114, 116, 126
New Cumnock   24, 27, *28*, 84, *85*, 98, 98, 101, 110, 112, 116, 119, 121, 126, 128, 135
New Luce   35
New Measurement Train   *15*, *111*, 126, *127*
Newcastle upon Tyne   69, 86, 94, 119
Newmilns   22, 56
Newton Junction (Ayr)   99, 112
Newton on Ayr   *18*, 38, *110*, 124
Newton Stewart   86
Newtonhead
Nobel's Explosives Works   71, 136, 137
North Ayrshire   7
North British Locomotive Company   141
North British Railway   43

Ochiltree   41, 42, 49, 51, 7, 145
Open Golf Championship   8

P & O   109
Paisley   60, 86, 90, 9
Pathfinder Railtours   125
Patna   31, 51, 52, 67, 129, 130, 133
Patterton   46
Pennyvenie   126, 133, 147
Pereceton   20, 136
Perth   62, 124
Pinmore   35
Pinwherry   35
Polnessan   31, *127*
Polquhairn Colliery   52, 72, 73

Polquhap Summit   *27*, 28
Portland, Duke of   10
Portpatrick   33, 116, *117*
Portpatrick Railway   29
Potterston Junction   131
Prestwick   14, *17*, 47, 56, 59, 69, *80*, 85, *90*, 98, 119
Prestwick Airport   8, 69, *91*, 98, *107*, 115, 119, 123, 128
Prestwick Town   98, 119
Purclewan Mill   131

Racks   27
Rail Express Systems   109
Railtrack   104, 116, 148
Rankinston   42, 50, 51, 52, 67, 71, 72, 73, 133, 135
Rankinston Viaduct   *49*
Ratcliff Power Station   122
Ravenscraig Steelworks   99
Renfrewshire   7
Riccarton   56, *57*, 57, 103, 117, *122*, 122, 136
Riccarton & Craigie   57
Rigg   27
Robert The Bruce   8
Royal Navy   69
Royal Troon Golf Club   8
Rugeley B Power Station   122
Ruston Hornsby   145
Ryeland   56, 69

Saltcoats   19, 91, *92*, 119, *120*, 123, 128
Saltcoats North   46, 67
Sanquhar   27, 119
Scarborough   86
ScotRail   89, 98, 104, 106, 109, 144
Scottish Coal   115, 121, 148
Scottish Industrial Railway Centre   *145*, *146*, *147*, 147, *148*, 149, 149, *150*, 150
Scottish Railway Preservation Society   125
Seamill   44
Second World War   69, 70, 71, 141
Sellafield   122
Sentinel locomotive   132
Settle & Carlisle Railway   37, 100, 125
Shankley, Bill   8
Shanks & Co.   136
Shewalton Moss   116, 137
Shilford Summit   37
Siemens   109
Sillyhole   129
Skares   41, 49, 112
Skelmorlie   7
Snodgrass   137
South Ayrshire   7
Speedlink   103
Springside   21, 128
Spyreslack Colliery   43
St Marnock (Kilmarnock)   *79*, 103, 116

Stena   109
Stevenson, George   11
Stevenston   *19*, 67, 68, 71, *111*, *122*, 136, 137
Stevenston Moorpark   46, 67
Stewarton   20, 37, 84, 96, 116, 117, *118*, 124, 126
Stewarton (Annick Water) Viaduct   *49*, 49
Stonebriggs   42
Stonehouse   43
Stranraer   7, 33, 35, 80, 86, 94, 96, 119, 124
Stranraer Harbour   109
Strathaven   43, 56, 69
Strathclyde Passenger Transport Executive   89, 94, 96, 106
Sturgeon, Nicola   8
Swindon   80
Swinlees Colliery   137

Tarbolton   38, *40*, 59, 69, *101*
Templand Viaduct   48, *48*
Templehill (Troon)   52
Thirdpart Junction   57
Thornhill   27
Torrance, Sam   8
Trabboch   41
Transport Scotland   108, 109
Transrail   109
Troon   8, 14, 46, 47, 52, *53*, *54*, 59, 64, 69, 85, 90, *94*, *107*, 115, 116, 119, *124*, *125*, *126*, 137, 141, *142*
Troon (Old)   *16*, *17*, *79*
Troon Harbour   13, 47, *55*, 56, 71
Troon Junction   52
Troon Templehill
Turnberry   8, 62, 63, 68, 73, 121
Turnberry Golf Club   8, 63
Turnberry Hotel   60, *62*, 63, 68

Uplawmoor   46

Wabtec Rail Scotland   143
Walker, Johnnie   7, 63, 103
Walter Alexander & Co.   142
Waterside   30, 31, *32*, 51, *105*, *129*, 129, 130, *130*, *131*, 131, 132, 135, 145, 147
Wemyss Bay   108
West Burton Power Station   12
West Highland Railway   124
West Kilbride   43, 44, 91, 121
Westminster   104
Whitecraigs   46
Whitehill Pit   42, 73
Wigtownshire   7
Wright, William   11

Yoker (Clydebank)   144
York   91, 125
Yorkshire   115